READING ASSESSMENT
IN AN RTI FRAMEWORK

READING ASSESSMENT IN AN RTI FRAMEWORK

Katherine A. Dougherty Stahl
Michael C. McKenna

THE GUILFORD PRESS
New York   London

© 2013 The Guilford Press
A Division of Guilford Publications, Inc.
72 Spring Street, New York, NY 10012
www.guilford.com

Printed in the United States of America

This book is printed on acid-free paper.

Last digit is print number: 9   8   7   6   5   4   3   2   1

Library of Congress Cataloging-in-Publication Data

Stahl, Katherine A. Dougherty.
    Reading assessment in an RTI framework / Katherine A. Dougherty Stahl, Michael C. McKenna.
       p. cm.
    Includes bibliographical references and index.
    ISBN 978-1-4625-0694-1 (pbk.)—ISBN 978-1-4625-0696-5 (hardcover)
    1. Reading—Ability testing. 2. Reading—Remedial teaching. 3. Response to intervention (Learning disabled children)—Evaluation. I. McKenna, Michael C. II. Title.
    LB1050.46.S73 2013
    372.48—dc23
                                                          2012010299

About the Authors

Katherine A. Dougherty Stahl, EdD, is Assistant Professor of Reading at New York University, where she serves as Director of the Literacy Clinic and teaches graduate courses. Her research focuses on reading acquisition, struggling readers, and comprehension. In addition to teaching in public elementary school classrooms for over 25 years, Dr. Stahl has extensive experience working with struggling readers in clinical settings. Recently, she conducted an evaluation of New York City's pilot RTI framework and has been designated as an investigator in the RTI Technical Assistance Center for New York State. Dr. Stahl also serves on the International Reading Association RTI Commission.

Michael C. McKenna, PhD, is Thomas G. Jewell Professor of Reading at the University of Virginia. He has authored, coauthored, or edited over 20 books and more than 100 articles, chapters, and technical reports on a range of literacy topics. Dr. McKenna's research has been sponsored by the National Reading Research Center and by the Center for the Improvement of Early Reading Achievement. He was a member of the National Reading First Expert Review Panel and has worked with Reading First teachers in eight states.

Preface

The importance of response to intervention (RTI) has never been clearer. We strongly believe that RTI, when fully implemented, represents our best hope of building the kind of schoolwide framework necessary for making truly informed choices about the type and intensity of the reading instruction children receive. When we wrote *Assessment for Reading Instruction, Second Edition* (K. A. D. Stahl & McKenna, 2009), our goal was to build a broad but practical foundation in assessment and provide a battery of informal measures that could be used to inform instructional planning. Our goal for this book is to offer the guidance needed to use these and other tools in an RTI framework. In both books, we organize assessment strategies around the cognitive model of reading assessment.

Several features of this book make it especially useful for educators who wish to implement a workable RTI framework or to refine a framework that is already in place. These features include:

- Consistent ties to our assessment text and to the reproducible measures contained there.
- Added reproducibles for recording data and conducting an assessment audit.
- Vignettes that exemplify the ideas contained in the chapters.
- Extensive web resources for locating information.
- Close connections with the Common Core State Standards.

We want to be clear that this is a book about the assessment component of RTI. We offer guidance and tools for gathering the information needed in an RTI framework. It is not, however, a comprehensive guide to RTI. We stop short of describing in detail the instructional approaches and programs that might be used in RTI. There are many resources already available for that purpose. Our work with schools has caused us to realize that it is the assessment component that is most problematic. And because assessment is the cornerstone of an RTI framework, it is important to get it right.

Getting assessment right requires both a clear idea of what an effective framework should look like and a practical philosophy about testing. Our own philosophy is simple and it has guided every aspect of this book. We believe that:

- An RTI framework must be lean and mean. It must be practical enough to be implemented yet thorough enough to inform choices about instruction.
- An effective framework must embrace the idea of tiers, through which teachers provide instruction of increasing intensity.
- Assessments should be guided by an overall strategy that identifies areas of need. For us, that strategy is the cognitive model.
- Classification of a child in special education should be a last resort, and the decision must be made on the basis of careful records as to what has been tried.

In Chapter 1, we address the inevitable question of how much assessment is needed. We discuss the need to strike a balance in what is asked of teachers, and we speak frankly about the diminishing returns of overassessment. We next introduce the principal kinds of assessments used in RTI. First, we distinguish between norm- and criterion-referenced measures. We then explore the idea of curriculum-based measures (CBMs) and their importance in an effective RTI framework. We examine the roles of various assessments and underscore how the same assessment can often serve more than one purpose. The importance of fidelity in giving and interpreting assessments is stressed. In Chapter 2, we take the long view of reading assessment, relating it to the expected development of young readers. Doing so requires an awareness that some skills, such as alphabet knowledge, are "constrained." That is, they are skills that teachers can expect to be completely mastered at some point. In contrast, assessments must also target "unconstrained" skills. Areas such as vocabulary continue to develop throughout the experience of schooling, and are never "mastered." In this chapter, we anchor our discussion in the cognitive model as we delineate all of the components of reading development into measurable parts. We examine how best to conduct assessment in order to get the answers required by RTI. In each instance, we explore how various kinds of assessments (norm referenced, informal, and CBMs) can complement each other within an RTI framework.

Chapter 3 describes an assessment audit. We outline the entire process of conducting an audit and provide forms for classifying assessments currently in use, identifying redundancies, and filling gaps in the assessment framework. We cast a wide net by including assessments given by special educators and other specialists. In a word, we start with *everything* in current use. We then prune the assessments back to a manageable number, plant additional assessments to fill gaps, designate the personnel who will be responsible for administering each assessment, and outline a plan for the professional development needed to ensure fidelity.

Chapters 4 to 6 address assessment at Tiers 1, 2, and 3, respectively. In Chapter 4, we focus on Tier 1 assessments—those used to screen entire grade levels and to identify early on those students who may require more targeted instruction. Here we speak about the relevance of informal reading inventories, group-administered spelling inventories, and related measures in following up on CBMs used to screen. We separately address how these instruments are used to assess foundational skills and conceptual vocabulary. In Chapter 5, we describe the standard protocol approach to RTI at Tier 2 and tell why we recommend this approach over its alternative, the problem-solving approach. We outline the assessments needed at this tier and offer specific ways to set goals and keep meaningful records. We distinguish between a child's level of performance and the rate of progress, and we take on the knotty issue of how many rounds of instruction are necessary before prudent decisions about responsiveness can be made. In Chapter 6, we take up the problem-solving protocol as a basis for conducting assessments of high-risk children. We discuss the assessments most useful in planning high-intensity instruction, and we address the interface between Tier 3 and special education. We offer strategies for making sense of complex arrays of data and approach the challenge of Tier 3 children from the standpoint of a mystery to be solved. We suggest important distinctions between assessing children in the primary and upper-elementary grades, and we close the chapter with the oft-neglected question of what happens when Tier 3 instruction is effective.

In Chapter 7, we offer specifics about how to set up and maintain a record-keeping system. We go beyond most treatments of this topic by suggesting how data kept on individual children can be aggregated to gain insights into how instruction at each tier and across grade levels is working. We discuss the important issues of who should bear the responsibility for administering and recording assessments. We next move to the use of data systems in reaching decision points for moving children across tiers, and we raise the issue of determining whether instruction has been provided with fidelity. We then turn to ways that data can be used as a vehicle for professional development, and we close with suggestions for reaching out to parents in an effort to keep them informed and to involve them as partners.

In Chapter 8, we tackle the job of actually implementing an RTI framework. We discuss a range of instructional approaches and interventions, though our discussion is an overview rather than a thorough treatment. The focus is on how to learn more about them. We next speak to the importance of professional development, which must include both a broad understanding of the rationale of RTI and the narrower knowledge of how to give and interpret specific assessments. This chapter contains an extended vignette of one elementary school's journey to full implementation of an RTI framework. We use its experience as a means of addressing two additional topics—the important role of coaching and suggestions for evaluating the effectiveness of an RTI framework.

We have tried our best to write a book that is both practical and specific, that reflects both research and common sense, that is consistent with standards, and that affords guidance in the issues central to RTI. We are committed to a belief that RTI represents the most promising means of providing appropriate instruction for children who struggle. If this book helps educators move closer to that goal, we will have succeeded as authors.

KAY STAHL
MIKE MCKENNA

Contents

CHAPTER ONE

Assessments in an RTI System

Fulfilling the promise of response to intervention (RTI) demands balance. Our idealistic notion of proactive, adaptive instruction must be weighed against the realities of schools and classrooms. In considering the detailed information offered by present-day assessments, we must weigh the time they require against the benefits we can expect from having given them. Although we adhere to the idea that assessments can guide our efforts to plan targeted instruction, we do not believe that more is always better. We have discovered that the benefits of RTI can be realized with no more than a simple set of informal assessments applied strategically.

That simple set of assessments must be chosen to help reach the following goals:

1. Quickly screen all students to determine areas of difficulty.
2. Follow up with diagnostic measures to help plan targeted instruction.
3. Periodically monitor progress to determine the near-term impact of that instruction.
4. Collectively aid in determining next steps.

Using assessments to achieve these goals requires a solid understanding of how they work and what they can tell us. It also requires a system that ensures their sparing and deliberate use, governed by a decision-making strategy that is clear to all.

THE ASSESSMENT DILEMMA: FINDING THE "JUST RIGHT" AMOUNT

The poet Robert Browning once offered this advice to painters: "Less is more." By that he meant that excessive detail often serves little purpose. We believe that, up to a point, this idea can be applied to reading assessment. Imagine a school where every child was given a full clinical battery of tests. Information would abound, and in a very few cases nearly all of it would be useful in planning interventions. However, for the vast majority of students, most of the information would reveal few unique insights essential for guiding effective classroom instruction. In our two university clinics, we occasionally encounter such students. They are referred by frustrated teachers or anxious parents, but they actually present simple profiles that extensive diagnostic assessments only confirm. In short, they are overtested.

An efficient RTI assessment system is lean and mean. It embraces a "Goldilocks" approach in which just the right amount of assessment is conducted to maximize student growth. The extremes are avoided. Too little assessment can result in vague guidance for teachers and instruction that is not sufficiently targeted. Too much assessment rarely results in those "aha moments" that provide the key to student success. Overassessing also requires time that might have been devoted to instruction. After all, during an assessment, the student is not learning and the teacher is not teaching. Unless the results offer practical insights into the kind of instruction that will serve the student best, this is a lose–lose situation.

Figure 1.1 shows the relationship between the amount of assessment we conduct and the amount of student growth we can expect on the basis of what we learn. This is not an empirical graph, but it represents, in a general way, our combined experience in classroom and clinic. In the early stages of assessment, the information we obtain about a child can be used to plan instruction that is likely to be far more effective than what we might have provided before the assessment. For example, determining an appropriate level of text would help immensely in placing the child in materials that will allow optimal progress. However, in giving additional assessments, we soon reach a point at which less and less useful information

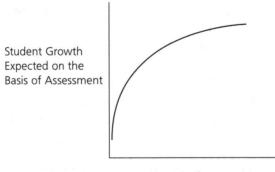

Student Growth
Expected on the
Basis of Assessment

Amount of Assessment

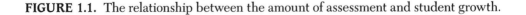

FIGURE 1.1. The relationship between the amount of assessment and student growth.

is obtained. The key is to find the point where we know enough to plan effective instruction.

THE ROLES OF ASSESSMENT IN RTI

If we are to conduct the "just right" amount of assessment—no less, no more—we need a system to direct our efforts. Of central importance in developing such a system is an understanding that assessments are of different kinds and serve a variety of purposes. Like tools, assessments are designed for specific functions. Using them for other purposes can be misleading and counterproductive. Unless you are like McKenna, for example, you would never use a wrench to do the job of a hammer.

Types of Assessments

To ensure a good understanding, let's begin with an overview of the principal kinds of assessments and how they might be used in an RTI system. From there, we'll review the uses of these assessments.

Norm-Referenced versus Criterion-Referenced Assessments

Test scores must be interpreted in order to make them useful. A score alone, without a frame of reference for interpreting it, has no meaning. As an example, consider an informal test designed to determine whether a child can apply the rule of silent *e* in decoding one-syllable words. Such a measure is one subtest of the Informal Phonics Inventory (Form 5.3 of *Assessment for Reading Instruction*, Second Edition [McKenna & Stahl, 2009]). The child views the following pairs of words:

| cap | tot | cub | kit |
| cape | tote | cube | kite |

For each pair, the teacher points to the upper word and asks the child to pronounce the lower one. ("If this is *cap*, what is this?") Scores on this subtest can obviously range from 0 to 4. But what does the score for a given child tell us? One way to give it meaning is to use a cutoff score, or criterion, to help us judge whether the skill assessed has been mastered. If we are satisfied with the criterion, the score can help us determine whether instruction in the rule of silent *e* is desirable. Another way to give meaning to the score would be to compare it to the scores of other children. Because this skill is typically taught in first grade, we could judge the score in terms of what is normal at a particular point in time. These two basic approaches to interpretation lead to different conclusions about test performance and they are intended to answer different questions.

CRITERION-REFERENCED TESTS

When the goal of assessment is to determine whether a skill has been mastered, a criterion-referenced assessment can be useful. For example, interpreting that portion of the informal phonics inventory that assesses the rule of silent *e* has an 80% criterion associated with it. If a student scores at or above this level, a teacher is justified in concluding that additional, targeted instruction in this skill is not required. Note that because only four items are administered, a perfect score is needed to denote mastery.

Criterion scores are useful in two cases. When assessing skills that are constrained (i.e., skills for which total mastery is possible), criterion scores can help determine whether or not mastery has been attained. The silent *e* subtest is a good illustration. When a child meets the criterion, the issue is settled. The second case involves a skill that is never totally mastered but for which we can establish criteria for specific points in time. We call such criteria benchmarks because they are determined through longitudinal studies designed to predict future performance. Tests of oral reading fluency, such as those included in Dynamic Indicators of Basic Early Literacy Skills (DIBELS) Next and AIMSweb, are examples of assessments for which shifting benchmarks provide useful gauges of a student's needs. The DIBELS Next benchmark for the Oral Reading Fluency (ORF) subtest in the fall of grade 2 is 53 words correct per minute (WCPM) for passages written at a high second-grade level. But in the fall of grade 5, the benchmark is 111 WCPM for passages written at a high fifth-grade level. Developmental shifts and text demands influence the formation of benchmarks for commercially produced tests.

To sum up, criterion scores can serve either as indicators of a child's mastery of constrained skills or as benchmarks that rise with time and task. In both cases, the measurement issue is between the child and the skill. The performance of other children on the assessment is not directly involved in interpreting the score.

NORM-REFERENCED TESTS

When the goal of assessment is to compare a child with the overall population of children, a norm-referenced test is appropriate. Here, a child's raw score is converted into one or more norms, which are converted scores used to make comparisons possible. Many norms are possible, but only a few are typically used in RTI assessments. Three of the most common are defined in Table 1.1, along with their strengths and weaknesses.

Now let's consider the example of oral reading fluency from a normative standpoint. According to the norms developed by Hasbrouck and Tindal (2006), a

TABLE 1.1. Characteristics of Common Norms

Norm	Definition	Advantages	Drawbacks
Percentile rank	Percentage of age peers that a child's score equals or exceeds	• Relatively fine grained	• Cannot be averaged • Are not linear, making gains hard to interpret
Stanine	One of nine statistically equivalent categories, with one lowest, five average, nine highest	• Ease of comparison, using two-stanine rule to judge significant differences	• This gross, at-a-glance measure may hide small differences and gains
Grade equivalent	Estimated grade and month associated with a test score	• Appropriate for some adaptive tests	• Easily misinterpreted • Usually computed by extrapolation rather than by assessing children at various grades • Discouraged by the International Reading Association

beginning second grader who reads 53 WCPM would score at the 50th percentile rank. This means that the child is exactly in the middle of the pack, dead average. This information provides a second frame of reference by which to judge performance based on that of other children; when available it can be considered in tandem with a benchmark (a cutoff score predictive of future success).

Curriculum-Based Measures

A curriculum-based measure (CBM) is a type of standardized test that is aligned with grade-level curriculum. The original CBM tasks were actually constructed using samples of a school's curriculum materials. However, today's CBMs are produced commercially to reflect different components of a grade-level curriculum area. The commercially produced CBMs are most popular because the resources invested in mass production increase the ability to provide tests that are *technically adequate*, meaning that they are valid and reliable. The tests are usually timed, enabling them to be sensitive to small margins of growth. Data from CBMs are easily summarized on charts and within web-based data management systems.

GENERAL OUTCOME MEASURES

General outcome measures (GOMs) are a type of CBM that assess the general outcome on a complex task that is not divided into subskills. For example, oral reading fluency and maze are designed to be GOMs of fluency and comprehension, respectively. Children are given reading passages that typically developing children would be expected to be able to read at the end of a particular grade level. GOMs are a means of looking at students performing a complex task when looking at individual subskills does not really portray the desired overall instructional goal. In order to read fluently, a number of foundational subskills must be operating together. GOMs assess this overall operation. However, if children are having performance difficulties, the GOM does not provide specific diagnostic information because it is designed to look at general overall performance on a capstone task.

SKILL-BASED MEASURES

Skill-based measures (SBMs) are similar to GOMs in that they measure sets of individual skills that are likely to be accomplished by the end of a school year. However, rather than the assessment requiring a single process that requires the interaction of multiple skills, each SBM is composed of mixed items from a set of goals. This type of assessment is commonly used in math to measure growth on individual computational skills across a school year. Each SBM might consist of a random collection of each type of computation that children are expected to master by the end of the year. As children improve over time, the total scores go up. However, items are keyed to particular skill areas and can be used to inform instruction.

MASTERY MEASURES

Mastery measures (MMs) are CBMs that measure discrete skills. For example, those CBMs that measure letter identification fluency or letter–sound fluency are considered MMs. They are useful when it is important to monitor a skill that is taught in isolation or while troubleshooting a particular area that is giving a student difficulty.

Functions of Assessment

In order for RTI to work, the assessments must serve a variety of purposes. They must quickly identify the existence of problems. They must help to identify specific deficits to be targeted through instruction. They must reveal whether students are responding to targeted instruction. Finally, they must produce long-term results useful in evaluation at the level of the classroom, the grade level, the school, and the district. These four functions are usually labeled as screening, diagnostic, progress monitoring, and evaluation.

Screening

Screening assessments are universally administered in an RTI system. They are either quick to administer (such as an AIMSweb or DIBELS fluency passage) or they already exist (such as an end-of-year achievement test from the previous year).

Because all students must be assessed, screening tests reveal only broad portraits of individual students. They lack sufficient detail to plan instruction. Their chief advantage lies in identifying students who are experiencing problems in a particular area. For those identified, a more fine-grained assessment is required, one designed to provide diagnostic information. Essentially, a trade-off is involved. What we gain in speed and efficiency, we lose in the specific information needed to plan instruction. Consider the DIBELS Next subtest Nonsense Word Fluency (NWF). In this test, a child pronounces rows of one-syllable pseudowords and is halted after a minute. Comparing the raw score (the sum of letter-sounds pronounced) against a benchmark can help determine whether basic decoding is a problem area. What it cannot do is identify specific skill deficits a teacher should address through instruction. We disagree with those who advocate inspecting individual nonsense words in an effort to determine these deficits (e.g., Hall, 2006). This is because the letter-sounds that make up the words are not presented systematically and also because the child's success or failure will depend in part on adjacent letter-sounds. For example, if a child pronounces *niz* by saying only the initial consonant, we cannot be certain that he or she has no knowledge of the sound /z/. This means that a follow-up assessment is needed, one that is designed to serve a diagnostic function.

Diagnostic

Diagnostic assessments provide information about a problem area in sufficient detail that targeted lessons can be planned. Because of the time they require to administer and score, they are not administered universally but only when screening has indicated a problem. Diagnostic testing is associated with a number of misconceptions. Teachers often believe that they are commercial tests that "come in a box," and are so involved that only specialists can administer and interpret them. Although a few diagnostic assessments are like that, the type most useful in RTI is informal and easy to give. Such a test yields information that is immediately useful in planning instruction. As one example, consider the Informal Phonics Inventory (McKenna & Stahl, 2009). After DIBELS NWF has indicated that a child is below the benchmark, the inventory can identify specific deficits. Because of the time required to give the inventory and because of the fact that many students do not exhibit problems with decoding, it is neither practical nor necessary to administer it to all students.

Assessments designed to diagnose rarely make good screeners. However, they are useful for targeting instruction. Without diagnostics, it would be difficult for teachers to plan deliberate interventions that can meet students' needs in the most time-efficient manner. Without diagnostics, instruction may address the general need without providing the specificity that facilitates accelerated growth. Skilled interpretation of the diagnostics allows teachers to teach only the content that is needed and to skip the instructional content that is already mastered or content that is beyond the students' zone of proximal development (ZPD)—that which they can do with assistance.

Progress Monitoring

Progress monitoring assessments are the mainstay of RTI. They are given periodically to determine whether a child is responding to the intervention provided. They are often alternate forms of the same tasks used as screening tests. Wixson and Valencia (2011) identify two types of progress monitoring tests: (1) formative tests, used to gather information while instruction is under way, and (2) summative tests, which are given for benchmarking purposes, typically in fall, at midyear, and in spring. Monitoring progress allows teachers to know when their instruction is working and when a course change is required. Progress monitoring scores can be recorded as a record of an individual's growth over time, and this record can be instrumental in deciding whether more intensive instruction is needed. These scores can also be averaged at the classroom, grade, and school levels to track success over time and from grade to grade. Assessments useful in progress monitoring include alternate forms of standardized instruments, such as those available from DIBELS and AIMSweb, but they can also include running records and teacher-constructed measures geared precisely to the content taught.

Evaluation

Evaluation assessments are aimed at determining whether teachers and schools are meeting the collective needs of students. The most prominent examples are undoubtedly the high-stakes assessments required by No Child Left Behind and other outcome tests. These tests are the "bottom line" of RTI and they serve the interests of some stakeholders. However, they tell us relatively little about individual students beyond a tentative screening function. More sensitive indicators of the health of an RTI program lie in the screening and progress monitoring measures. When scores are examined collectively, the "state of the school" can be described in considerable detail (Walpole & McKenna, 2012). For example, the percentage of children at risk should fall throughout the year if they are responding to the intervention they receive. Scores on screening and progress monitoring measures can be examined by teacher and grade level to help coaches identify priorities. We return to this idea in Chapter 8.

Function versus Type of Assessment

A frequent confusion about the basic functions of assessments is the belief that a particular test can have only one function. The problem with this belief is that the same test can often serve several functions. Table 1.2 lists examples of familiar tests

TABLE 1.2. Examples of Familiar Tests and the Functions They Can Serve

Test	Screening	Diagnostic	Progress monitoring	Outcome
DIBELS Next	✓		✓	✓
AIMSweb	✓		✓	✓
Informal Phonics Inventory		✓	✓	✓
Inventory of High-Frequency Words		✓	✓	✓
Running Record of Text Reading (K–2)	✓	✓	✓	
Group Achievement Test	✓			✓

and the functions they can serve. Although we might argue about whether a certain test can serve a certain function, there can be no disputing that many (perhaps all) tests can serve more than one.

Using Tests in Tandem

Using screeners to identify problem areas and diagnostics to narrow those areas to practical instructional targets is the great one–two punch of assessment-driven instruction (McKenna & Walpole, 2005). Once targeted instruction begins, progress monitoring tests come into play, helping us gauge the extent to which the instruction is having the desired effect. Figure 1.2 illustrates the decision-making process that is guided by the results of all three types of assessments. Note the return loop back to targeted instruction when progress monitoring indicates that the problem persists. This pathway is central to RTI, for it reflects an awareness that a child is not responding and requires that targeted instruction be reconsidered.

Summative and Formative Uses of Tests

The terms *summative* and *formative* are an occasional source of confusion. The difference lies in how the results are used. Formative assessments yield results that are used to modify instruction. Progress monitoring is a type of formative assessment because the results may cause a teacher to alter an approach or to change course entirely. Summative assessments, on the other hand, are used to ground judgments after the fact. They may result in big-picture changes, such as whether a particular intervention program is effective or whether special education staffing is called for, but they are not used to make day-to-day judgments about what kind of instruction to provide. A comparison with cooking is sometimes used to explain the difference:

> *When the cook tastes the soup, that's formative.*
> *When the guest tastes the soup, that's summative.*

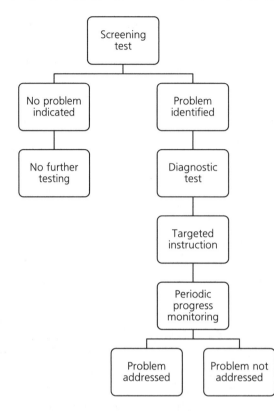

FIGURE 1.2. How different assessments are used to target instruction.

ENSURING FIDELITY

The elegance of an RTI assessment system lies in using the least amount of testing to make prudent decisions for every child. Making sound decisions based on a small number of tests requires that they be administered, scored, and interpreted properly. Every test involves a small amount of measurement error, and our goal must be to keep that error as small as possible. When guidelines are not followed, we increase the magnitude of the error and bad decisions can result. To illustrate how important the three dimensions of fidelity can be, let's consider the example of the DIBELS ORF subtest.

Fidelity to Administering an Assessment

Fidelity in administering the ORF requires that three passages be administered, that the child be stopped 1 minute into each passage, and that only the middle score be recorded. We have known teachers to take the tempting shortcut of giving only one passage. In doing so, they are gambling that the passage they choose is representative of the child's actual fluency level. On the ORF the one passage selected may be higher or lower than the child's true score. Although it is true that none of the three scores is likely to be a perfect reflection of the child's proficiency, we can have greater confidence in it because it fell between two other scores. Consider a beginning fourth grader who takes one DIBELS passage and scores 78. The teacher correctly judges the child to be performing below the benchmark (90). But what if the teacher were to administer two more passages, as the instructions indicate, and the child scores 90 and 95? In that case, the middle score would have been at benchmark and the teacher would have reached the wrong conclusion.

Another example involves gaming the test to improve the apparent level of performance. We have known a few teachers, under pressure to produce results, who have encouraged children to skip unfamiliar words during ORF testing. Because only the number of words correctly pronounced are counted—and not the errors—directing students to skip words rather than "lose time" attempting to decode them, leads to inflated scores. Such scores can hardly be the basis for sound decisions regarding the kind of instruction children should receive.

Fidelity to Scoring an Assessment

Fidelity to scoring is obviously important as well, but there are many ways to go wrong. On the ORF, the teacher might miscount the number of words attempted, undoubtedly the most common mistake. It is also possible that synonyms and other semantically acceptable substitutions might be counted correct (saying *dog* for *pup*). This practice seems reasonable and was once supported by some theorists, but it has now been shown to be misleading (McKenna & Picard, 2006/2007). More important, it was not used to determine the DIBELS benchmarks and can only inflate a child's score, leading to overestimates of proficiency. The teacher might also count all of the words attempted up to the 1-minute mark, including errors. Doing so would result in a measure of rate (WPM) rather than in the combined measure of rate and accuracy (WCPM). Rate alone is a limited and outdated measure of fluency. And once again, the DIBELS benchmarks are based on WCPM, which requires scoring on this basis alone. Yet another threat to fidelity is the temptation to give the benefit of the doubt. We all want our students to do well, but when we catch ourselves saying, "He's just having a bad day—I know he knows that word and I won't count it wrong," we are jeopardizing the results of the assessment.

In short, scoring fidelity can be compromised by a number of factors, some accidental, some deliberate. Everyone makes mistakes, to be sure, but teachers can minimize them by carefully reviewing scoring procedures and adhering to them. There are good reasons for doing so.

Fidelity to Interpreting an Assessment

Fidelity to interpretation depends on the nature of the test. For criterion-referenced tests, strict application of the mastery criteria or benchmarks is important. We don't mean to suggest that there is no room for professional judgment, and we have already acknowledged the part played by measurement error. It is prudent to think of a "gray area" just below the criterion and to use other information about a child's performance to interpret scores falling there.

In the case of a mastery test, such as those that make up the Informal Phonics Inventory, we have set the criterion at 80% but have created a zone just below it to indicate partial mastery. A child's performance can be categorized as follows:

Mastery	80–100%
Review	60–79%
Systematic Instruction	Below 60%

The "review" category creates a gray zone, created to avoid the all-or-nothing judgment that a mastery criterion implies.

In the case of a benchmark test, like ORF, there is also a gray area. Imagine that our beginning fourth grader had a middle score of 88. The benchmark for the beginning of fourth grade is 90, and technically the child is below benchmark. Is further consideration warranted? This is a judgment call for teachers seeking to form flexible groups for targeted instruction. DIBELS approaches the issue by establishing three levels of risk, often color coded as green, yellow, and red. This child would be placed in the yellow zone on computer-generated reports, but it is still left to the teacher to decide on an instructional course of action.

For norm-referenced tests, careful consideration of what the norms actually mean is required. Unlike a criterion-referenced test, which comes with well-defined scores for categorizing a child's performance, a norm-referenced test is more complicated. As we have said, there are several norms from which to choose, and each comes with unique methods of determining the gray area. Fortunately, however, such tests are not a major component of RTI. Their chief utility lies in end-of-year outcome assessments, such as nationally normed group achievement measures, and in the assessments given by special educators to determine the appropriateness of a particular category (e.g., learning disabled).

CHAPTER TWO

Assessing Reading Development

Reading development is the accumulation and coordination of many subskills. Our cognitive model of assessment (McKenna & Stahl, 2009) posits that reading comprehension is dependent upon (1) automatic word recognition, (2) comprehension of the language of the text, and (3) the ability to use the strategies needed to achieve particular purposes for reading (see Figure 2.1). Each of these three

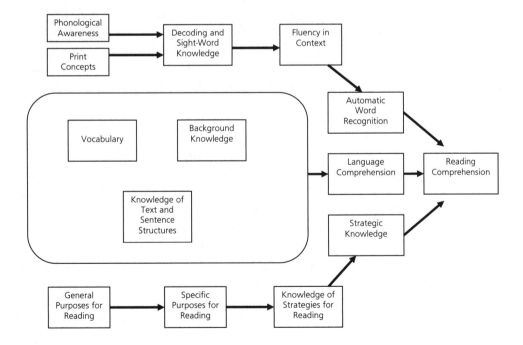

FIGURE 2.1. The cognitive model of reading assessment (revised 2009). From McKenna and Stahl (2009). Copyright 2009 by The Guilford Press. Reprinted by permission.

constructs might be further divided into particular subskills. Automatic word recognition requires fluent reading of connected text, which is in turn dependent on decoding abilities, automatic identification of high-frequency words, print concepts, and phonological awareness. Background knowledge, vocabulary, and knowledge of syntax contribute to language comprehension. Purpose-setting and comprehension strategies, such as monitoring, taking stock, and visual imaging, are essential strategic elements in the meaning-making process. While most teachers would agree that the primary purpose of reading is comprehension, the time allocation in many classrooms, especially primary classrooms, tends to privilege components that contribute to automatic word recognition.

Not surprisingly, in many RTI frameworks, the assessment of reading subskills underlying automatic word recognition dominates the assessment system. There can be no doubt that these skills are necessary to a child's development as a reader, but to devalue other components of reading, such as vocabulary and comprehension, is shortsighted. All components of the cognitive model should be assessed, at least at the screening level.

NEW VISIONS OF READING DEVELOPMENT: CONSTRAINED AND UNCONSTRAINED SKILLS

We suspect that another reason for focusing on the lower-level skills is that there is an end in sight! After all, there are only so many letter sounds and a limited number of high-frequency words. Likewise, concept of word is a skill that once mastered is over and done. By the same token, phonological awareness does not expand indefinitely but is an attainment that has a clear closure. Skills of this sort are constrained by their very nature, and their instruction has a beginning and end. Not so in the case of higher-level skills. There are always new word meanings to learn and more complex texts to comprehend.

This distinction between constrained and unconstrained skills is now central to the way we think about reading assessment. Constrained skills theory (Paris, 2005) suggests that there is a continuum of skills, with some, such as letter knowledge and word-recognition abilities, more tightly constrained than others, such as comprehension and conceptual vocabulary (see Figure 2.2). The most tightly constrained abilities consist of a discrete number of items (e.g., letter names) resulting in mastery within a relatively short time period. Because everyone tends to master constrained abilities, there is variability among students only within a short window of time. The constrained, discrete nature of these skills makes them easier to teach and assess than comprehension, which is multidimensional and complex. Because proficiency in the unconstrained abilities varies by text complexity, purpose for reading, genre, and instructional context, no single assessment is adequate for measuring these abilities.

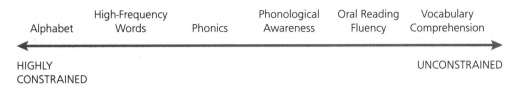

FIGURE 2.2. Continuum of constraint.

So while assessments of easily quantifiable constrained abilities may be used to screen young children for potential reading difficulties, we must be careful that assessment and instruction of constrained abilities don't dominate school literacy programs. An overemphasis on constrained skills in the primary grades may result in immediate spikes in CBMs and other discrete measures of constrained abilities, but in the long run the more complex skill areas will suffer if neglected. It makes no sense to believe that giving priority to constrained over unconstrained abilities will result in later success in comprehending a range of texts. To put it another way, constrained abilities are necessary but not sufficient for proficient reading. As early as kindergarten, the Common Core Standards (2010) are dominated by an emphasis on unconstrained skills. Although foundational skills are specified for each grade level, kindergarten through fifth, the number and depth of skills to be mastered in the areas of conceptual vocabulary, comprehension of literature, and comprehension of informational texts far outweigh the foundational skills.

Rather than simply adding or eliminating assessments to ensure a balance of constrained and unconstrained skills within a school RTI implementation, the faculty should first audit all reading assessments currently being given. The details describing how to conduct such an audit are provided in Chapter 3. Either before conducting the school assessment audit or simultaneously, a review of the assessments described below is useful. For a more thorough review and access to specific assessments, see McKenna and Stahl (2009).

ASSESSING AUTOMATIC WORD RECOGNITION

Phonological Awareness

Phonological awareness is the understanding that words are made up of abstract sound units. A phoneme is the smallest unit of sound in a spoken word. This awareness is entirely auditory and is not associated with written language in any direct way. It is not the same as phonics, which is the recognition of sound and letter relationships. The terms *phonological awareness* and *phonemic awareness* are sometimes used interchangeably, but there is an important distinction. Phonological awareness is the broader term. It incorporates sensitivity to word duration, rhyme, syllables, phonemic awareness, and manipulation. Phonemic awareness concerns phonemes alone, those individual sound units that are the building blocks of all spoken words. Converging evidence indicates that (1) instruction can improve children's phonological awareness and (2) there is a strong causal link between phonological awareness and later abilities in phonics and spelling (National Institute of Child Health and Human Development, 2000). According to the research, comprehensive programs that lasted less than 20 hours were more effective than longer programs. As with other constrained skills, more is not better and the content of instruction should be determined by diagnostic assessment. Then instruction should be carried out in small homogeneous groups in tandem with instruction about letters.

Curriculum-Based Measures

Many CBMs of phonological awareness are in current use. We describe here two of the more common and useful types.

FIRST SOUND ISOLATION

One important reading prerequisite is a child's ability to isolate the first sound of a word from the rime (S. A. Stahl & Murray, 1994). In this CBM task, the examiner calls out a word (*boat*) and the child must say the beginning sound of the word (/b/). The score is the number of correct beginning sounds identified by the child within 1 minute. DIBELS Next recommends that this task be administered at the beginning of kindergarten and again at midyear.

PHONEME SEGMENTATION

Both DIBELS Next and AIMSweb test for the development of phonological awareness using a phoneme segmentation task beginning at midyear in kindergarten and extending through the middle (AIMSweb) or the end of first grade (DIBELS Next). The task requires children to isolate and say each phoneme in the words presented by the examiner. If the examiner said "cat," the child would be expected to say "/k/ /a/ /t/." The children do not see the words in print; it is purely an auditory task. The score is the number of sounds that the students segment within 1 minute. According to S. A. Stahl and Murray (1994), the learning trajectory for segmentation begins with separating onsets from rimes. At a more advanced level, children can segment words like *cat*, with consonant–vowel–consonant patterns. Finally, they can segment the phonemes represented by consonant blends, such as *brat* and *tent*. As with any general outcome screening measure, diagnostics will be needed to determine where the process is breaking down for a child who is not functioning at a proficient level, particularly those children who cannot yet understand or perform the segmentation task.

Word	Child says	Score
flat	fl at	2/4
cash	k a sh	3/3
lamp	l a p	3/4

Informal Measures

The ability to segment each individual phoneme in a word is developmentally more advanced than other earlier-developing phonological awareness tasks (S. A. Stahl & Murray, 1994). Therefore, many young children may not possess the phonological awareness needed to be successful with segmentation. Informal measures can be useful in determining how far their awareness has developed.

PHONOLOGICAL AWARENESS LITERACY SCREENING

Phonological Awareness Literacy Screening (PALS; Invernizzi, Swank, Juel, & Meier, 2007) comprises a set of assessments that may be administered in a small group and individually to children in the primary grades. It assesses abilities that tend to develop earlier than phoneme segmentation. PALS-PreK includes a rhyme identification subtest and a beginning sound isolation subtest. PALS-K (for students in kindergarten) assesses rhyme identification and beginning sound identification. PALS 1–3 (for students in grades 1 through 3) includes an individually administered blending task and aural sound–letter identification task requiring children to segment words and identify the letters that represent particular sounds.

HEARING SOUNDS IN WORDS

Hearing Sounds in Words (Clay, 2006; McKenna & Stahl, 2009) is a sentence dictation task that requires the analysis of invented spelling. Clay's version has been normed with 5- and 6-year-old children. In addition to a quantitative score, this task provides a window for viewing phonological awareness, print concepts, and alphabetic knowledge. Therefore, this instrument could measure multiple constructs in an early literacy test battery.

SPECIFIC PHONOLOGICAL AWARENESS TASKS

Specific phonological awareness tasks (McKenna & Stahl, 2009) can be done in a gamelike format and documented on an as-needed basis. Today, by the time most children enter kindergarten they have mastered rhyme identification and rhyme generation. However, when children are unable to perform the segmentation task, it is a good idea to assess the prerequisite phonological awareness tasks, such as word duration, number of beats (syllables) in a spoken word, rhyme identification, rhyme generation, and blending a series of dictated phonemes that form a word (examiner says "/c/ /a/ /t/," child says "cat"). An individual student checksheet is useful for documenting the constellation of phonological awareness abilities including the ability to isolate the beginning phoneme from the remainder of the word, identify a common phoneme in a set of words, categorize a set of words with a common phoneme, and perform manipulations to a word such as adding and deleting phonemes.

Normed Measures

Kits are also available for assessing phonological awareness and using a norm to compare children's performance by age and grade level. The Test of Phonological Awareness (TOPA-2+; Torgesen & Bryant, 2004) assesses children in kindergarten through second grade on initial and final sound categorization and invented spelling of nonsense words. The Comprehensive Test of Phonological Processing (C-TOPP; Wagner, Torgesen, & Rashotte, 1999) is suitable for testing individuals from 5 to 24 years of age. It consists of subtests in blending, sound matching, rapid naming, and segmentation. The C-TOPP is particularly useful for determining the strengths and weaknesses of older students who still appear to be having difficulty in this area. Finally, the Woodcock–Johnson III Normative Update Tests of Achievement (WJ III NU ACH; Woodcock, McGrew, & Mather, 2001, 2007) subtests assess blending, invented spelling, rhyming, and manipulation.

High-Frequency Words

Immediate recognition of the most frequently occurring words in the English language is an important contributor to fluent reading. Since over 80% of running words in texts are made up of the most frequently appearing 500 words, recognizing these words with automaticity can increase the likelihood of proficiency in reading fluency. Therefore, it is a constrained reading skill that should be tracked in the early grades. If children are not meeting fluency benchmarks in the intermediate grades, examining knowledge of high-frequency words is a good diagnostic starting point.

Curriculum-Based Measures

Word identification fluency is not currently measured by AIMSweb or DIBELS Next. However, Intervention Central (*www.interventioncentral.org*) makes it possible to generate your own randomly selected lists based on the Dolch Word List. To create a CBM, you simply select the entire Dolch Word List option or an individual-level designation (preprimer, primer, first, second, third) and the number of words that you wish to be displayed. The website will create a random list of high-frequency words based on your specifications.

Informal Measures

High-frequency words can also be tested by using the original Dolch or Fry word lists (McKenna & Stahl, 2009). Selecting subsets of 50 to 100 words from these lists and testing children diagnostically, will provide a precise list of words to be explicitly taught to each child. The Fry List is sequenced by order of frequency in the English language. The Dolch List (Dolch, 1936) is based on the words that commonly appeared in children's reading books during the 1930s. Words not recognized automatically need to be explicitly taught and drilled.

Normed Measures

The Test of Word Reading Efficiency (TOWRE; Torgesen, Wagner, & Rashotte, 1999) is a test that measures the accuracy and efficiency of sight word and nonsense word reading for anyone between the ages of 6 and 24. The TOWRE's Sight Word Efficiency task is a list of words that students read in 45 seconds. Raw scores are then converted to scale scores, percentile ranks, and age and grade equivalents. This is particularly useful when working with dysfluent older readers who appear to know the 300 most frequent words. Although this subtest doesn't provide information about exactly what words to teach, the comparison to a norm allows a teacher to determine whether a student's level of automaticity with high-frequency words is comparable to other readers of the same age. The translation to scale scores also allows a teacher to compare a student's competency with high-frequency words to decoding ability. Therefore, a teacher can determine if oral reading fluency is being compromised equally by the component skills or whether instructional interventions should target one or the other with more intensity. Consider Bethany, who enters fourth grade reading 52 WCPM, or just above the 10th percentile rank (Hasbrouck & Tindal, 2006). She scores at the 46th percentile rank on the TOWRE Sight Word Efficiency subtest, but only at the 11th percentile rank on the TOWRE Phonemic Decoding Efficiency subtest (nonsense words). These results indicate that there is no need for further isolated sight word diagnostics or interventions. Rather, Bethany's intervention specialist should apply more specific decoding diagnostics and devote a portion of the intervention time to teaching explicit decoding strategies, as well as providing Bethany with opportunities to apply these strategies while reading connected text.

Word Recognition and Related Alphabetics

Curriculum-Based Measures

LETTER-NAMING FLUENCY

Both AIMSweb and DIBELS Next include a test of letter naming. Children in kindergarten and early first grade (fall) are asked individually to identify as many upper- and lowercase letters as possible within 1 minute.

LETTER–SOUND FLUENCY

AIMSweb also includes an individually administered test of letter–sound fluency that requires children to identify the sounds made by single letters in isolation. This test is administered in the winter and spring of kindergarten and in the fall of first grade.

NONSENSE WORD FLUENCY

DIBELS Next and AIMSweb assess application of phonics knowledge and decoding abilities through the use of a nonsense word measure that is administered individually from the winter of kindergarten through the end of first grade (AIMSweb) or fall of second grade (DIBELS Next). These tests only test knowledge of short-vowel nonsense words with single-consonant onsets and endings.

Informal Measures

UNTIMED SYSTEMATIC MEASURES OF LETTER NAMES AND LETTER SOUNDS

These are a part of most early literacy assessment packages or they can be easily constructed. As a highly constrained skill set, the measurement net used in a CBM or a teacher-constructed task is quite small and consists only of a small number of items. The term *measurement net* refers to the size and nature of the sample a measure collects. A test covering letter names or individual letter sounds casts a smaller measurement net than a test of high-frequency vocabulary. Therefore, individual letter names and letter sounds are typically mastered within a small window of time, especially if explicit instruction targets the set of unknown items indicated by assessment results.

PHONICS

On the other hand, phonics inventories look quite different and provide far more detail about the content of instruction than a nonsense word test. The nonsense word test is useful for determining if a child can apply phonics to novel words. However, it doesn't provide a deliberate system of organizing the phonics content for determining student strengths and weaknesses. Although some have argued that phonics measures like the DIBELS Next NWF subtest can be closely inspected in order to identify specific skill deficits (e.g., Hall, 2006), we do not recommend this approach. The representation of skills is random, analysis of them would be time consuming, and the results could not be easily integrated into the kind of record-keeping system needed in RTI. Instead, we prefer direct measures of phonics skills. These are easy to administer and have an obvious link to instruction.

Research indicates that the most effective phonics instruction is explicit, systematic, and targeted to students' developmental needs (National Institute of Child Health and Human Development, 2000). Organized developmentally, good phonics inventories provide insight into where the child is along the word-recognition development continuum (Bear, Invernizzi, Templeton, & Johnston, 2011; Ehri, 1998). A good phonics inventory will provide teachers with the knowledge of which skills have been mastered, which require review or consolidation, and which call for explicit instruction.

A number of inventories are available for this purpose. For example, the Informal Phonics Inventory (McKenna & Stahl, 2009) begins by testing each consonant letter sound and each blend in isolation. Next, it assesses each final blend embedded in a single-syllable word and then moves to increasingly difficult vowels. Reflecting typical development, it begins with a collection of words with short-vowel sounds, moves to words with a silent *e* and then tests each vowel digraph, diphthong, and *r*-controlled vowel. Similarly, the Z-Test is a list of the most frequently occurring phonograms (rimes), organized by increasing difficulty (McKenna & Stahl, 2009). Automatic recognition of these patterns is essential for formulating over 500 one-syllable words and many of the syllables encountered in multisyllabic words. The Informal Decoding Inventory (Walpole, McKenna, & Philippakos, 2011) is likewise based on the typical sequence in which decoding skills are acquired. It uses real and nonsense words to place a child within this sequence: short vowels, consonant blends and digraphs, *r*-controlled vowels, silent *e*, and vowel teams.

Normed Measures

The TOWRE Phonemic Decoding Efficiency subtest (Torgesen et al., 1999) is a normed test of nonsense word reading that is individually administered. It requires the child to read a list of two- to six-letter nonsense words in 45 seconds. Although normed for individuals between the ages of 6 and 24, this specialized assessment is most usefully applied with children in the intermediate grades and above who are encountering sustained difficulties in word recognition and fluency.

The WJ III NU ACH (Woodcock et al., 2001, 2007) Basic Reading Cluster assesses foundational reading skills. Administered individually in a tightly standardized format, the results have high reliability and validity. Additionally, the WJ III NU ACH can provide important data in a potential special education referral. For this reason, it is likely to be used only in Tier 3.

Spelling

Curriculum-Based Measures

AIMSweb includes a spelling CBM. It may be administered individually or to a group. After a word is dictated, children have 10 seconds (7 seconds in grade 3 and up) to spell the word. There are two scoring options for spelling CBMs (Hosp, Hosp, & Howell, 2007). In the first option, students receive a point for each word spelled correctly in every detail. In the second option, a method called correct letter sequences (CLS) is used. CLS is the total number of pairs of letters that are in the right sequence. Although correct letter sequences are more sensitive to improvement, they are more time consuming to score and require more training and attention to fidelity of scoring. The level of attention to detail makes mistakes more likely. See Table 2.1 for examples of CLS scoring.

If constructing your own spelling CBMs, Hosp and colleagues (2007) suggest that words be drawn from the comprehensive spelling curriculum for the year. Every test must include the exact same number of letters in order to see growth from test to test. They recommend using 12 words for first and second grade and 17 words for third grade and above. As with any general outcome measure, spelling CBMs are "not intended to make specific statements about how the student is currently performing on a daily or weekly lesson or unit, but to be able to make broader statements like: What is this student's level of general spelling skills compared to other students, or is this student progressing sufficiently in spelling?" (Shinn & Shinn, 2002, p. 7).

Informal Measures

We are strong advocates for using one of the systematic measures that enables teachers to determine each child's stage of spelling development. A longstanding and robust body of research has determined that children's spelling follows a

TABLE 2.1. Examples of CLS Scoring

Dictated words	Possible CLS	Student response	CLS	WSC
funny	□f□u□n□n□y□	□f□u□ny□	4/6	0
wouldn't	□w□o□u□l□d□n□' □t□	□w□od□nt□	4/9	0
Sunday	□S□u□n□d□a□y□	su□n□d□a□y	4/7	0

clear developmental trajectory (Henderson, 1981; Invernizzi & Hayes, 2004; Read, 1971). Assessments by Bear and colleagues (2011) and Ganske (2000) provide reliable, quick, and easy measures of these developmental stages. For example, on the Elementary Spelling Inventory each word is more difficult than the previous word and contains features than can be analyzed to determine what the child understands about the English alphabetic system (Bear et al., 2011). Analysis of the test items can be used to make decisions about what spelling skills have been mastered, require review, or require systematic instruction. Then a scope and sequence of instruction is recommended with the pace dictated by ongoing criterion measures and progress monitoring. Additionally, Bear and colleagues provide a qualitative scale that allows teachers to examine student compositions so that a comprehensive evaluation may incorporate not just how students are performing on a spelling test but also whether they are applying their knowledge in consistent ways during the writing process. Recommendations for instruction always incorporate active engagement with patterns in reading and spelling. Unlike the CBM that simply tells you whether a student is making strides generally, a developmental spelling assessment can be used in tandem with corresponding materials. By closely linking assessment with instruction, teachers are in a position to know exactly what a child needs to learn next and how to teach it.

Normed Measures

Norm-referenced tests of spelling are available but their utility is limited. Some group-achievement measures, such as the Stanford Achievement Test (Harcourt Brace Educational Measurement, 2002), contain spelling subtests that can be administered as early as grade 2. These could be used as a screening measure *if* the test is already given as a matter of policy. However, we cannot recommend that a group spelling measure be administered just for this purpose. It is true that normative data might be useful in tracking spelling proficiency across the year, but this goal can also be accomplished by compiling the results of a developmental spelling assessment to gauge the movement of groups of children from one stage to the next.

Some individual measures, such as the WJ III NU ACH (Woodcock et al., 2001, 2007), contain spelling subtests. As we have mentioned, however, instruments of this kind are used primarily in a problem-solving protocol and for special education referrals. As part of a comprehensive profile for an individual student, spelling norms could be useful in making comparisons between subtests.

Fluency

In the last decade, fluency has shifted from the most "neglected reading goal" (Allington, 1983) to a reading priority surrounded by controversy. Everything from its definition to the best way to assess it to its impact on later reading has been a source of contention. We find the definition established by Kuhn, Schwanenflugel, and Meisinger (2010) to be useful:

> Fluency combines accuracy, automaticity, and oral reading prosody, which, taken together, facilitate the reader's construction of meaning. It is demonstrated during oral reading through ease of word recognition, appropriate pacing, phrasing, and intonation. It is a factor in both oral and silent reading that can limit or support comprehension. (p. 240)

This definition incorporates the traditional components of accuracy, automaticity, and prosody, but it also considers the role that these factors play in service to comprehension. Therefore, if applying this fluency construct, the most valid assessment would need to incorporate measures of prosody and comprehension in addition to accuracy and rate.

There has been a trend to use rate and accuracy as proxies for general reading ability. These two contributors are necessary but not sufficient for comprehension. When the assessment and instruction of fluency are confined to these two factors, the reader's focus on rate often leads to quick, monotone reading that may actually interfere with comprehension processes.

Additionally, there have been challenges with prosody measurement. Prosody's ambiguous chicken–egg relationship with comprehension diminishes the value of its measurement in the eyes of some experts. In the field of speech and language, spectrographs have been used to measure the prosodic features of spoken language. They have also been used in recent studies of reading prosody (Benjamin & Schwanenflugel, 2010; Miller & Schwanenflugel, 2008). More typically, however, teachers use rating scales to describe students' expression, phrasing, pacing, and intonation, an approach also used by the National Assessment of Educational Progress. Although researchers report moderately high interrater reliability (79–86%) using these scales, it is unlikely that school faculty could achieve such levels without extensive training, using anchor recordings of oral reading and frequent booster sessions (Klauda & Guthrie, 2008; Rasinski, Rikli, & Johnston, 2009).

Curriculum-Based Measures

DIBELS Next and AIMSweb measures of oral reading fluency are widely used and often required in RTI frameworks. These tests are administered from mid-first grade until sixth grade in DIBELS Next and from mid-first grade until eighth grade in AIMSweb. Students are given 1 minute to orally read each of three grade-level passages. The score is the number of words read correctly in 1 minute. The median of the three scores is identified as the student's score. Prosody is not measured;

these tests only incorporate rate and accuracy. DIBELS Next requires that children perform a retelling of each text for 1 minute after they read the passage. The retelling score is the number of words spoken. The website offers three reasons for requiring a retelling score. One is that it makes educational sense to gauge fluency only when a child is reading for meaning. Fluency is, after all, in service to comprehension, and treating fluency checks like speed drills can be misleading for teachers and send the wrong message to students. A second reason is that more of the variance in scores is accounted for when retelling scores are included. This fact makes them more predictive. Finally, the developers of DIBELS Next argue that strong evidence of reliability and validity underlie the use of retelling scores. The question of reliability was a point of contention when retelling was introduced in the original DIBELS system, but the DIBELS Next developers claim that these criticisms have been addressed. Teachers already familiar with DIBELS may dispute the need for a retelling measure, and in fact the benchmark passages can be administered and scored without retelling. However, use of the DIBELS Next database requires that a retelling score be submitted along with the fluency score for each student. The reason for this requirement is that a formula is used to compute a composite score, and the retelling score is a part of that formula. AIMSweb, in contrast, does not incorporate any follow-up measure of comprehension. As with other measures from these publishers, scores are translated into risk categories and also a percentile rank (Daniel, 2010; see also Chapter 1). AIMSweb reports also translate performance into Lexiles, which correspond roughly to the level of text complexity appropriate for a child.

It is important to keep in mind that these measures of fluency are designed to be administered using grade-level texts regardless of the child's instructional reading level based on a comprehensive reading inventory that includes an analysis of both accuracy and comprehension. There are several reasons for this policy. One is that it employs a consistent measure of how the child is performing on grade-level material, and progress toward grade-level performance can be charted over time. A second reason is that fluency benchmarks have been established on the basis of grade-level texts. Asking children to read easier materials simply because they are at the instructional level would mean that the benchmarks could not be used. However, the disadvantage is that because the struggling readers are asked to read material at their frustration level, their typical orchestration of reading processes may be compromised causing a double jeopardy effect on rate and accuracy. This is one of many reasons why it would be inappropriate to do a diagnostic miscue analysis on a CBM passage.

Advocates for the exclusive use of CBMs suggest using a range of CBMs to determine instructional level (Hosp et al., 2007). They suggest that a student's instructional level is the highest-level text at which the student's performance matches the norms for average rate. As an example, let's return to Bethany, our entering-fourth grader. Assume that Bethany's DIBELS Next ORF score is 48 WCPM, well below the benchmark of 90 for the beginning of grade 4. Let's further assume that she is also tested out of level, with easier passages. Her score for reading third-grade passages is 55, still below the third-grade benchmark of 70. At second grade, her score is 60, which at last exceeds the benchmark of 52 WCPM. Based on these results, we would judge Bethany's instructional reading level to be third grade (Hosp et al., 2007).

Informal Measures

RECORDS OF ORAL READING

Both running records and oral reading records on informal reading inventories may be timed to provide a WCPM score. Unless the amount of time a student reads is exactly 1 minute (as it is in DIBELS Next and AIMSweb), you will need to correct for the actual time. The following formula can be used to calculate WCPM regardless of how long the child reads:

$$\text{WCPM} = \frac{\text{Total number of words read correctly} \times 60}{\text{Number of seconds the child reads}}$$

The result can then be compared to a norms table such as the one prepared by Hasbrouck and Tindal (2006) to interpret the scores and to compare each student to national peers at the same grade (see Table 2.2). These records of oral reading should be conducted at a minimum on instructional-level text (90–94% accuracy and above 75% comprehension) for everyone and ideally on a range of texts to determine independent and frustration levels for struggling readers. Seeing how students perform on the range of difficulty levels enables teachers to target instruction more effectively and also see how processing behaviors shift as the child moves from easier to more challenging texts.

ASSESSING LANGUAGE COMPREHENSION

The three components of oral language development are vocabulary, background knowledge, and knowledge of text and language structures. These areas demonstrate the characteristics of unconstrained abilities. Unlike constrained skills, they are not linear sets of skills that are either known or unknown. Competency varies by purpose for reading, genre, text complexity, task, and instructional context. Assessment of background knowledge and facility with text and language structures

TABLE 2.2. Hasbrouck and Tindal's (2006) Oral Reading Fluency Norms for Grades 1–8

Grade	Percentile	Fall WCPM	Winter WCPM	Spring WCPM
	90		81	111
	75		47	82
1	50		23	53
	25		12	28
	10		6	15
	90	106	125	142
	75	79	100	117
2	50	51	72	89
	25	25	42	61
	10	11	18	31
	90	128	146	162
	75	99	120	137
3	50	71	92	107
	25	44	62	78
	10	21	36	48
	90	145	166	180
	75	119	139	152
4	50	94	112	123
	25	68	87	98
	10	45	61	72
	90	166	182	194
	75	139	156	168
5	50	110	127	139
	25	85	99	109
	10	61	74	83
	90	177	195	204
	75	153	167	177
6	50	127	140	150
	25	98	111	122
	10	68	82	93
	90	180	192	202
	75	156	165	177
7	50	128	136	150
	25	102	109	123
	10	79	88	98
	90	185	199	199
	75	161	173	177
8	50	133	146	151
	25	106	115	124
	10	77	84	97

is fairly elusive. At this point in time, the best measures for classroom purposes may be a combination of vocabulary assessment and informal observation during instructional interactions.

Although conceptual vocabulary abilities are unconstrained, the utilization of multiple measures can provide some windows into this area. However, teachers and other stakeholders must recognize that due to the unconstrained nature of vocabulary, assessment measures are not likely to display the clean linear sequence and mastery associated with constrained abilities. The context-dependent, incremental nature of vocabulary development is unlike the development of alphabet knowledge or phonics skills. This fact has important implications for assessment.

Standardized assessments may provide a baseline measure of global abilities through comparison with a norm, but they lack the sensitivity to inform classroom instruction (National Institute of Child Health and Human Development, 2000). These assessments cast a very wide measurement net. To put the problem another way, vocabulary screening measures do exist and they can help determine whether vocabulary is a weakness. However, diagnostic tests of vocabulary, which would identify the specific words we need to teach, do not exist. There are simply too many words and little agreement on which are most important. Therefore, the National Reading Panel recommended teacher-constructed assessments to match specific instructional goals and units. This recommendation has important implications as schools develop a comprehensive assessment system. Schools need to be cautious in selecting and developing assessments for vocabulary. A simplistic single-dimensional test is at best a quick fix for a multidimensional ability. Vocabulary (like comprehension) requires an attack on multiple fronts. Schools need to undertake a deliberate study of the kinds of constraints necessary for test reliability while still maintaining construct validity. How can words be selected and the degree of student knowledge be quantified so that there is consistency and cohesion within a school while providing for the incremental, nonlinear nature of word learning? This challenge is best addressed through deliberate professional development and school learning communities rather than by purchasing a commercial vocabulary program that is disconnected from the language needs that are associated with a school's existing curriculum.

Curriculum-Based Measures

A group of researchers have been testing the use of vocabulary CBMs by constraining the word corpus to science and social studies key vocabulary found in the most commonly used commercial textbook series (Espin & Deno, 1993a, 1993b, 1994–1995; Espin, Shin, & Busch, 2005). Most recently, Vannest, Parker, and Dyer (2011) developed a CBM system for multiple science units each of which consists of four sets of five probes for five key vocabulary terms. Sets of probes are cloze tasks that require children to correctly match one of five related words to the correct application of the term or the definition of the term. We have included an example of each type of item below.

Condensation is the process of a gas changing into a liquid state. (Definition)

Small particles of water on the outside of a cold drink are an example of *condensation* (Application)

These tests are computer reliant for both item generation and administration. Vannest and colleagues (2011) did not impose time limits in their study. This work is still in its nascent state. However, with the increasing popularity of CBMs and the technology capacity of larger commercial test producers such as DIBELS Next and AIMSweb, it seems likely to us that widely available CBM tests for vocabulary may be on the horizon. Likewise, it would not be surprising if future vocabulary CBMs were timed.

Informal Measures

High levels of construct validity can be guaranteed if schools use vocabulary measures that come with their reading series or create assessments that are matched with a corpus of vocabulary that are essential to their science and social studies curricula. Assessments such as the Vocabulary Knowledge Scale, the Vocabulary Recognition Task, and the Vocabulary Assessment Magazine are just a few of the research-based assessments that can be used to document vocabulary development that is tied to a school's existing curriculum. Each of these measures is context situated and considerate of incrementality and depth of knowledge about tested words. For a full discussion of these assessments and the application of criteria for evaluating vocabulary assessment in general, see Pearson, Hiebert, and Kamil (2007) and K. A. D. Stahl and Bravo (2010).

Normed Measures

Peabody Picture Vocabulary Task IV

The Peabody Picture Vocabulary Test–IV (PPVT-4; Dunn & Dunn, 2007) is an individually administered receptive vocabulary test for Standard American English. It is based on a universal vocabulary corpus. It may be used from preschool through adulthood. The administrator says a word and presents a page containing four pictures. The test taker must identify the picture that is associated with the word. Typically, each administration takes from 15 to 20 minutes. The norming sample for this edition of the PPVT matches the U.S. Census for gender, race, region, and socioeconomic status. Additionally, it has been conormed with the Expressive Vocabulary Test. All reliability and validity coefficients are above .90.

Expressive Vocabulary Test, 2nd Edition

The Expressive Vocabulary Test, 2nd Edition (EVT-2; Williams, 2007) is an individually administered measure of expressive vocabulary and word retrieval for Standard American English. It may be used from preschool through adulthood. It can be used as the expressive companion to the PPVT-4. Test takers are shown a picture and must provide a name for the picture. Like the PPVT-4, the norming sample matches the U.S. Census for gender, race, region, and socioeconomic status. Reliability coefficients are at or above .90 for all age groups.

ASSESSING READING COMPREHENSION

It is not an easy job to assess students' comprehension because the processes that students use to comprehend a text can only be measured indirectly with evidence that is reflected through some other ability such as oral language or writing. Typical of an unconstrained skill, competency varies by purpose for reading, genre, text complexity, task, and instructional context. If one knows the phonogram *eet*, it is easily identified and pronounced whether reading a caption book or a medical journal. However, such is not the case for comprehension abilities. Being able to identify the key ideas or generate inferences in one text does not mean that one is capable of performing that skill in a text of a different level, different genre, on a different topic, or in a different context. As a result, the assessment of comprehension needs to be multifaceted. At a minimum, both reader-generated responses (such as retellings or written summaries) and question answering are necessary to measure various facets of comprehension. An evaluation of a student's comprehension should never be based on a single task.

While the student's ability to recount and answer questions about the text can provide clues about comprehension, these tasks don't really provide information about the possible hurdles to a student's comprehension. Other formats such as maze tasks and multiple-choice tests provide even fewer clues. Measures based on these tasks can do no more than screen. If screening reveals a problem, the RTI system suggests following up with a diagnostic assessment. However, there are currently no diagnostic tests of comprehension, although they have been attempted in the past. The problem is that comprehension subskills are so highly correlated (Schell & Hanna, 1981). Inferring a sequence is inseparably entangled with inferring a cause-and-effect relationship, and so forth. There is, however, a diagnostic *process*, and the process is reflected in the cognitive model. If we refer back to Figure 2.1, we see that comprehension is not broken down in comprehension subskills but into the components necessary for comprehension to occur. The assessment process entails examining these components to determine areas of weakness. In this chapter, we have explored how assessments can help us determine whether comprehension difficulties might stem from word recognition and vocabulary.

To these we might add proficiencies along the lowest tier of Figure 2.1. Successful readers establish purposes for reading and apply useful strategies in order to make sense of texts. Therefore, if successful decoders with strong language skills are encountering comprehension difficulties, one might consider performing diagnostic assessments that tap into strategy use and purpose for reading (Jacobs & Paris, 1987; McKenna & Stahl, 2009).

Curriculum-Based Measures

Most schools that use CBMs in the upper grades to measure comprehension use a maze task (Fuchs & Fuchs, 1992; Shapiro, Zigmond, Wallace, & Marston, 2011). A maze task consists of grade-level passages in which every nth (often seventh) word is deleted after a complete, uninterrupted first sentence. The examinee selects a word that will make sense in the sentence from three or four choices displayed in bold text. Maze can be thought of as a timed, multiple-choice variation of the cloze task. As such, criticisms of the cloze task apply to maze. Shanahan, Kamil, and Tobin (1982) demonstrated that the ability to fill in a cloze blank does not rely upon making sense of the total passage, but is confined to comprehension at the sentence level. This fact poses a threat to test validity because it is in direct conflict with modern theories of comprehension (K. A. D. Stahl, 2009). On the other hand, cloze tests are highly correlated with less contentious comprehension measures (McKenna & Layton, 1990), so the objections to cloze and maze testing are probably overstated.

The maze task is appealing for several reasons (Shin, Deno, & Espin, 2000). It does not rely on questions, which involve a host of assessment issues, and is easy to administer and score. It can be administered in an individual or group setting, manually or on a computer. Depending on which commercial package is used, students are allotted either 1 minute or 3 minutes to read each passage. The multiple-choice format makes it easy to score. The variations in maze construction may cause variations in sensitivity, reliability, and validity. Care and deliberation in the selection of passages is crucial. The passages should be between 100 and 400 words long to allow for internal coherence (Parker & Hasbrouck, 1992). Passages for younger students would be likely to be at the lower end of this range. Since progress is reflected in gains, passages should have approximately the same readability. Based on these construction complexities, the use of commercial packages is advised. DIBELS Next Daze passages range from grades 3 through 8. AIMSweb maze passages are available for students in grades 1 through 8. Additionally, AIMSweb reports translate students' maze scores into reading levels expressed as Lexiles.

Informal Measures

For the youngest readers in kindergarten through second grade, students might be expected to retell the events or information in the text. Additionally, a few literal and inferential questions might be asked (Goldman, Varma, Sharp, & Cognition and Technology Group at Vanderbilt, 1999). However, generally before mid-second grade texts do not have enough grist to support an extensive analysis of high-level comprehension. The whole point of early readers is that they are based on simple story lines involving familiar themes. Especially in kindergarten and first grade, it is most important to do a through miscue analysis to determine if the reader is orchestrating meaning, syntactic, and alphabetic (visual) systems to generate an oral reading that makes sense while looking right. While learning how to apply the alphabetic system to approach novel text, we want to continue to confirm that novice readers know that the primary goal of reading is to make sense of text. Documentation of this process can happen through the miscue analyses conducted on running records, documenting simple retellings, and anecdotal notes.

Certainly during kindergarten and first grade, extensive comprehension instruction should be occurring during teacher read-alouds and shared reading. In response to the text complexity demands of the Common Core Standards, schools are likely to expand the range of texts that even the youngest children are responsible for comprehending. Because of decoding limitations in the early grades, it is likely that high-level comprehension will surround texts that have been read to them or with them. In our work with schools, we have found that most schools do not have the human resources available to conduct individual assessments of listening comprehension in the primary grades. Children's foundational literacy abilities at this level would inhibit their ability to fully reflect their reading comprehension of a complex story or informational text. In order to obtain a valid, reliable measure of comprehension, both retelling and question answering would need to take place orally on an individual basis (Goldman et al., 1999). So although this needs to be happening instructionally in the primary grades, it is unlikely that most schools can bear the burden of deep comprehension diagnostics and interventions except in the most extreme cases.

As readers grow in sophistication and the texts become more complex (beginning around mid-second grade), more intentionality in assessing each student's ability to retell and answer literal and inferential questions about a piece of text needs to be applied. A school should use a professionally developed assessment kit or informal inventory system with graded passages followed by a scale for scoring each component of a retelling and questions about each passage. The materials should contain multiple forms of passages at each level with at least two forms of narrative and informational text at each reading level. These measures allow for a more nuanced analysis of a student's comprehension strengths and weaknesses with a range of texts. The school assessment audit is a good time to evaluate the rigor of the existing informal comprehension assessment measure. Rather than a simple rating scale, the retelling scores should be based on points for specific story grammar elements, episodes, or idea units. Questions should require students to recall, interpret, integrate, and critique material in the text. This is a good time to compare how closely informal measures are explicitly aligned with the demands of the Common Core Standards.

Normed Measures

A wide range of group-administered normed tests are available to measure comprehension across the grade levels. Standardized tests such as Terra-Nova, Stanford 10, the Iowa Tests of Basic Skills, and the Gates–MacGinitie Reading Tests are among the most commonly used. Most contain passages that are followed by comprehension questions. Typically, the group-administered tests use a multiple-choice format. Many newer tests allow for constructed responses and expanded responses to a range of questions. For example, the Stanford 10 may be administered from K to 12 and the questions tap into literal understanding, interpretation, critical thinking, and strategy application. Typically, listening comprehension is tested in kindergarten, and basic comprehension in first grade may require the students to match a picture to a simple, short text passage (MacGinitie, MacGinitie, Maria, Dreyer, & Hughes, 2006). These tests identify how a student compares to other students at a similar age or grade level. They are in fact designed for making such comparisons, and for this reason they can function as effective screening measures within an RTI framework.

Group achievement tests of comprehension do not, however, work well as diagnostic assessments. We strongly discourage attempts to analyze student performance on the basis of the *kinds* of comprehension questions missed. One reason for caution is that there are typically too few items for reliable measurement. Another, as we mentioned earlier, is that item clusters tend to be too highly correlated to offer useful insights about comprehension (Schell & Hanna, 1981). An exception involves comparisons of literal and inferential comprehension. Items assessing these two global areas are correlated, to be sure, but not highly enough to make comparisons pointless. The Comprehension subtest of the Stanford Diagnostic Reading Tests (SDRT; Karlsen & Gardner, 1995) categorizes questions in this way and generates both a literal and inferential score.

Additionally, the WJ III NU ACH (Woodcock et al., 2001, 2007) is an individually administered test that measures both listening and reading comprehension. Many of the subtests in the WJ III NU ACH are presented within clusters, allowing for intra-ability and intraindividual analysis. This does allow for a detailed diagnosis of an individual's strengths and weaknesses within a specific domain such as comprehension.

CHAPTER THREE

Conducting a School Assessment Audit

Accountability in our schools has led to the ongoing addition of tests over time. In moving toward the implementation of an RTI system, most schools should conduct an audit of the existing assessments being used at each grade level. In this way, a school can create a cohesive system of assessment, determine where there might be redundancies, or where voids exist that might need to be filled. The audit process also opens the door for conversation among faculty members about values and beliefs related to assessment, the roles of faculty in implementing the components of the assessment system, and the expertise of faculty in administering and interpreting assessments, as well as the means of communicating the results among stakeholders.

GRADE-LEVEL AUDIT OF CURRENT ASSESSMENTS

The first step in the assessment audit is for each grade level to list all assessments currently being administered by each team member at that grade level. See Form 3.1 at the end of this chapter. At this stage, teachers simply list and describe what various members of the team currently use. What we have recently discovered in many schools is the ongoing addition of multiple tests over several years without eliminating tests. As a result, multiple tests are being used to assess the same constructs, and instructional time is lost as a result. The reasons for adding more and more tests vary. Adopting new programs may mean new assessments. Often, teachers on the same grade-level team may use different tests to assess the same construct depending on when they were hired. In other cases, teachers may simply be unaware of the redundancy or are reluctant to give up a particular assessment once it has become part of the routine. Inconsistencies in assessment procedures and reporting forms often exist both horizontally (within a grade) and vertically (between grades). The function of the assessment audit is to reveal current assessment practices in a school. The process involves gathering information and is nonjudgmental. The audit itself does not involve changes in the assessments used, but the results are essential in constructing a school's comprehensive RTI assessment system.

Identifying the Assessments Currently Administered

In the first column of Form 3.1, teachers at each grade work together to list each assessment that is administered throughout the year, including standardized state tests. The person(s) administering these tests is recorded in column two. Depending on a school's schedule and infrastructure, reading specialists and English learner (EL) specialists may participate in grade-level team meetings or complete their own form independently for each grade level at which they teach. However, it is important that every teacher participate in the audit process.

Constructs

Next, the fundamental constructs being tested are identified. For example, the preliminary construct of a phonics inventory is word recognition in isolation. The oral reading portion of an informal reading inventory (IRI) is likely to be used to assess both word recognition and fluency if the reading is timed. The retelling and the questions following the oral or silent reading of an IRI are both used to assess reading comprehension. List each component of a multicomponent assessment like the IRI separately. Hence, one assessment may be used to inform multiple constructs or it may be necessary to use multiple assessments to inform different dimensions of a single construct. The fact that both retelling and question answering are used to assess comprehension does not indicate redundancy because they assess different dimensions of comprehension. The same is true for word recognition. The miscue analysis of oral reading indicates what a child attends to as he or she orchestrates multiple cueing systems. On the other hand, the phonics inventory provides a teacher with systematic, comprehensive information about the specific patterns that have either been mastered, require review, or require explicit instruction with intense practice. So although they are both measures that contribute to a teacher's knowledge about a child's degree of control over word-recognition processes, they are not redundant.

Function

Next, identify the function served by each test. Screening tests are brief assessments in a given area and are used to develop a preliminary indication of which students may be at risk for reading difficulties or who may require accommodations well above grade level. Diagnostic tools provide a more precise picture of a student's reading and writing skills after screening has indicated a problem. These assessments identify strengths and weaknesses in particular skill areas. Diagnostic assessments are used to inform instruction in precise ways. A progress monitoring tool is a brief assessment that may be used to determine whether an individual student is making adequate progress toward a particular learning objective. An alternative form of a screening instrument is often used for this purpose. These assessments are given frequently and need to be sensitive to growth within short learning intervals. As a result, they are often timed. Their use is coordinated with instructional approaches or interventions to give teachers an idea of whether these approaches are working. For this reason, progress monitoring assessments are at the very heart of RTI. Finally, outcome measures are assessments that are commonly administered on a group basis at the end of a year or at the end of a unit.

The most efficient assessments can be used to fulfill multiple functions. For example, the first-grade application of the Benchmark Assessment System (Fountas & Pinnell, 2010) or some other commercial system of benchmark-leveled text reading can be used as a screening device to identify which children are performing below level, it can be used diagnostically to form small instructional groups, and it can be used to monitor a student's growth in reading increasingly difficult text at accuracy rates of 90% and above.

Training

Finally, the teachers will identify the level of training that has been made available for each assessment. At the most basic level, a formal introductory training for each assessment should have been conducted. If commercially produced CBMs are being used, then in order to check off "introduction" it is necessary for each teacher who administers the tests to have received formal training from a certified DIBELS Next or AIMSweb trainer. These sessions are frequently conducted at central locations for several schools, or a certified trainer may have been hired by the school to conduct professional development for the school staff members. Alternatively, a school or district may have sent a person for the extended certification training. Preliminary training by a certified trainer is necessary to ensure that particular attention has been drawn to the nuances of each assessment compared to other similar assessments that may be familiar to the teachers. Additionally, training by the certified trainer includes the use of anchor readings for scoring and activities to ensure tester-to-tester reliability. In our work with schools, it is common to hear teachers complain about test results that appear off-target, from testing conducted the previous year or in other settings. Formal training with certified trainers is the first step toward achieving reliable data.

Formal introductory training must be conducted with any assessment that a school decides to adopt as part of their assessment system. Even something as basic as a high-frequency word-list test needs to be administered, scored, and reported in a standardized format within a schoolwide assessment system. A school's literacy coach, reading specialist, literacy team leader, or special education leader might conduct these training sessions. The transition to an RTI paradigm is a good time for a school to clean up and systematize how assessments are administered, scored, and reported. The audit might reveal that teachers on a particular team are all administering the same tests in a common way, but that they are recording the data differently, ranging from scraps of paper to computer spreadsheets. In an RTI paradigm, reliance on data is crucial. Therefore, it is imperative that schools move to a uniform, clean, efficient system for data management. We have found that grade-level audit conversations expose each team's assessment beliefs as well as the status of the assessment system.

For assessments to yield accurate results, testers must employ standardized administration procedures. To ensure the standardization of procedures, fidelity checks of the assessment procedures should be conducted during each assessment cycle. Both DIBELS Next and AIMSweb provide checklists to ensure that standardized procedures are being followed throughout a school. For other measures, a school literacy team may want to construct fidelity checksheets. Although this can become burdensome if taken to the extreme, for complex measures with extensive consequences it is essential to verify that results are reliable. Literacy coaches, reading specialists, or peer teachers may conduct fidelity checks. For example, some of the teachers performing an audit recently complained about the unreliability of their students' text-level reports from the previous teacher. Although teachers had been trained to administer running records of oral reading in August, they did not use fidelity checksheets to ensure that a teacher's familiarity with her students did not result in a "drift" from standardized test-administration procedures in June.

Teachers at this school also noted during the audit process that they had not participated in booster sessions for running records or IRI procedures. Booster sessions are brief refreshers provided to review standardized assessment procedures, particularly those tricky components of the test administration. For example, for this particular test do we wait 1 second, 3 seconds, or 5 seconds before providing a child with an unknown word during oral reading? Are word additions scored as errors? Booster sessions are conducted periodically throughout the year, often immediately before a major test cycle (e.g., August, January, May). Typically, the school literacy specialist, literacy coach, or some other in-house faculty member with assessment expertise conducts the refresher booster sessions.

SUPPLEMENTARY SUPPORT ASSESSMENT AUDIT

It was surprising for us to observe that in many schools the special education teachers, EL support providers, speech teachers, school psychologists, and other support faculty were not included in school conversations about literacy assessments. In our model, everyone in the school must be included in this process. At this stage of RTI implementation, assessments are not owned by any group of teachers. The function of assessments is to measure student achievement and growth, inform instruction, and report student outcomes to a variety of stakeholders. In our model, school staff members share responsibility for these functions—and the knowledge they provide—jointly and with transparency.

For an effective assessment system with a supportive infrastructure to be formed, we believe in beginning with an audit of everything that exists and then pruning, nurturing, and designating. The necessity of total school involvement requires visionary leadership. Although school principals may know less about reading instruction than some of the school's teachers, RTI's reliance on infrastructure and professional development makes the principal the key player in this process. The principal sets the tone that ensures that teachers are working collaboratively as a collective unit rather than in separate silos. While there are certainly state and district-mandated policies that may influence assessment decisions by the various branches of support staff, those mandates must be conveyed in a respectful, transparent, inclusive way during the audit process. For example, if there are particular diagnostic tests that the district special education office requires special educators to use for annual reviews, those assessments need to be reported on the assessment audit. Likewise, if school psychologists use particular tests to identify a reading disability, all of those tests must be recorded as part of the assessment audit.

ANALYZING FOR VOIDS AND REDUNDANCIES

Each faculty member completes the audit worksheet after a short professional development session describing the components in each column. Often a literacy coach will conduct a brief (20–30 minutes) whole-school professional development session describing the components of the audit sheet. A meeting of all faculty also serves as a way of communicating the school's commitment to an RTI assessment system. It is an opportunity for the principal in particular to voice support and clarify expectations. The whole-school session is followed by personnel breaking into grade-level and support teams to complete the audit worksheet (45–60 minutes). After completing the worksheet, each team analyzes voids and redundancies.

Voids

It is easiest to identify voids among assessments currently in use. By looking at the columns that indicate constructs currently being tested, teams can identify holes in their assessment system. In doing so, it is helpful to keep in mind the relative importance of constructs at various grade levels. Conceptual vocabulary development, for example, is a goal at every grade level. This vocabulary is typically introduced during read-alouds, shared reading of complex texts, and themed or content-area instruction (e.g., units on plants or cultural traditions). In kindergarten and grade 1, assessment might take the form of conversation checksheets, word-wizard charts, and knowledge rating scales (see Blachowicz & Fisher, 2009). In the intermediate grades, testing of conceptual vocabulary might occur in paper-and-pencil formats, including analysis of constructed responses in unit tests, matching or cloze items in textbook vocabulary tests, or application of concepts in other written products that have been systematized by grade level to ensure accountability for key concepts (see K. A. D. Stahl & Bravo, 2010).

Despite its importance, conceptual vocabulary is frequently absent from a school's assessment battery, especially in the early grades. There are several reasons for this unfortunate gap. The most important is that schools do not have adequate vocabulary assessments because they lack a coordinated approach to instruction. This is true even though it is well known that struggling readers fall further and further behind. Andrew Biemiller (2012) states the problem in the bluntest terms: "Vocabulary levels diverge greatly during the primary years, and virtually nothing effective is done about this in schools" (p. 36). It is our hope that an assessment audit will be a first step toward addressing this problem. Another reason for the assessment gap is that vocabulary is hard to measure (National Institute of Child Health and Human Development, 2000; K. A. D. Stahl, 2011), and all of the approaches in current use have shortcomings (Pearson et al., 2007). Because vocabulary is unconstrained, it does not fit into the neat boxes we use for phonics and other foundational skills. Growth is incremental and continues on a lifelong trajectory. Moreover, word knowledge is rarely a matter of simply associating a term with a definition. Almost all words have multiple meanings and nuances, and a child's schema for a word becomes deeper and more complex over time (Beck, McKeown, & Kucan, 2002; S. A. Stahl & Nagy, 2006). In sum, the obstacles to vocabulary assessment are indeed formidable, but they do not justify excluding vocabulary from the assessment system. Far better to operate with imperfect assessments than to tolerate this gap and function in the dark. Collaborative discussions during the audit process enable teachers to define the existing voids and to become invested in creating solutions that will be used to measure student growth and inform instruction.

Testing of particular constructs will vary by grade level. In kindergarten, it is essential for Tier 1 and Tier 2 to have screening, diagnostic, and progress monitoring measures in place for phonological awareness. However, in second grade and beyond it is likely that only special educators and Tier 3 interventionists will be applying tests of phonological awareness with a small subset of struggling readers. Grades 2 and beyond should have a "not applicable (NA)" in the phonological awareness box. If second-grade general education teachers are conducting tests of phonological awareness with all children, it is likely that this test is adding unnecessarily to the assessment burden without paying off in achievement benefits. When an effective infrastructure for communicating assessment results exists, it is possible to streamline the number of tests being administered. This is why our model insists on audit participation by every faculty member in a school.

Additionally, if a test is used for screening purposes but doesn't diagnose what needs to be taught, there is a void even though the box may be checked. For example, a timed CBM of nonsense words may be administered as a test of decoding skills. Because it is a GOM, such a CBM can serve as a temperature gauge, indicating that decoding is or is not on target at a particular point in time. However, it cannot be used to plan instruction. A systematic, comprehensive diagnostic phonics tool must be administered to identify the particular patterns that have been mastered, require review, or need intense, explicit instruction (see McKenna & Stahl, 2009). Typically, this form of diagnostic would be administered only to students in a high-risk category. However, schools with adequate resources could administer this diagnostic to all students to ensure that children who are functioning above grade level are receiving instruction that will enable them to make 1 year of growth. Moreover, a K–5 RTI perspective demands that decoding growth be charted into the upper elementary grades, where the ability to decode multisyllabic words and to apply morphological analysis becomes critical but is rarely addressed (Walpole et al., 2011). If a school is in a situation in which children are reaching standardized achievement adequate yearly progress (AYP) goals, but not growth goals for children in the most proficient categories, this would be a necessary addition.

The Special Case of Oral Reading Fluency

In completing the audit checklist, you may be tempted to record a gap for diagnostics in the case of oral reading fluency. Assessment systems like DIBELS Next and AIMSweb do an excellent job of providing a screening tool for fluency, but neither offers a follow-up diagnostic. This does not mean that there is a gap, however. We have already discussed how comprehension assessment lacks diagnostic tests. The cognitive model suggests a *process* instead, through which contributing factors are considered. The same is true for oral reading fluency. When students fall below the fluency benchmark, the diagnostic process involves examining the two major contributors to fluency: sight words and decoding proficiency.

Redundancies

Because there may be multiple dimensions of a single construct being assessed, it is sometimes difficult to identify when more than one test is testing the same dimension. Consequently, more than one check in a column does not necessarily indicate a redundancy. In the previous example, a nonsense word CBM and a phonics inventory both measure decoding ability but they are not redundant. However, if classroom teachers are using DIBELS Next nonsense word measures and an external SWAT team assesses children using AIMSweb nonsense word measures, the situation would be redundant because the two tests are essentially the same but produced by different companies. Occurrences like this speak to the importance of all school faculty participating in the school assessment audit process.

Often, redundancies occur when different people who work with the same children are performing different assessments that may be serving the same function. Additionally, though the use of a SWAT team may be a time-efficient way to administer screening assessments, we have found that if the classroom teachers are simply handed the results, it is too easy for those results to be placed in a notebook without being used as intended. Disregarding test results compiled by others may lead to teachers readministering a similar test that is already familiar to them and that serves a similar function. In addition to ignoring test results stored in a notebook, a similar situation can occur when both the Tier 2 intervention teacher and the classroom teacher are progress monitoring oral reading fluency even though one may be using DIBELS Next passages and the other is using a different commercial program or online resources. These measures target the same proficiency and constitute redundant assessment. The audit process can expose these redundancies.

AFTER THE AUDIT OF EXISTING ASSESSMENTS

Once the audit has been conducted, it is time to begin a process of pruning, planting, designating, and nurturing. This process is best accomplished by grade-level teams with the support of a person who works across grade levels to help realize the ongoing schoolwide vision of the RTI process. This person might be a literacy coach, an RTI design team leader, a university-based critical friend, and assistant principal or principal. The process is likely to require multiple team meetings, and support staff might be called on to join particular meetings.

Although cumbersome, it is important for classroom teachers to have a voice in this process. When particular assessments are simply assigned, people tend not to value them or to be committed to using them. The assessment process simply becomes one more task to be checked off. In contrast, these conversations ensure that teachers see the value of the assessments in increasing student achievement and streamlining instruction. It is also professionally broadening to learn about a range of assessments and the belief systems associated with them.

Prune

First, get rid of the assessments that have been found to be redundant. Select the best one or the one that is consistent with the majority of the other assessments in use. For example, if your school has purchased a contract with AIMSweb, then use the assessments that are part of that package. Eliminate the DIBELS Next or other measures that some individuals may be using. If teachers in the upper grades are using the Qualitative Reading Inventory and the lower grades are using a combination of the Basic Reading Inventory (Johns, 2011) and the Benchmark Assessment System (Fountas & Pinnell, 2010), it will be important to look analytically at the characteristics of each and commit to one that meets the needs indicated by the audit. Teams should use the components of the audit as talking points in the deletion and selection process. In terms of functionality, construct, and training for reliability, which one is likely to be most efficient? Which assessment is most closely aligned with the demands faced by students on the state assessments? This conversation and the decision-making process result in faculty investment in the assessments that become a part of the schoolwide assessment system.

Plant

Next, add assessments or reporting systems that appear to be missing. For example, the primary-grade teachers who were all using the Dolch High Frequency List, but without any systematic framework, implanted an assigned list for each grade level and a common spreadsheet for reporting the results. Focusing on the automatic reading of the words in 1 second also required that some teachers prune back the expectation that children would write the words correctly as they learned to read them.

Other additions might be more extensive and require a phased approach. In keeping with the metaphor, these additions amount to planting seeds. For example, filling the conceptual vocabulary void might require more time and research by a school. A school might commit to being more mindful about how they currently teach and assess vocabulary, and even how they select important vocabulary during Year 1. As part of the process, a school faculty might commit to engaging in sustained professional development about vocabulary in Year 1, cleaning up the assessment of more constrained abilities, and committing to the development of a system for conceptual vocabulary in Year 2 after the prerequisite self-study and professional development. This is a smart solution because it allows for deliberation and investment by the faculty as opposed to purchasing a program that promises a quick fix for a complex ability.

Designate

Once the necessary assessments have been agreed upon, it is important to determine who will be responsible for administering particular assessments. Figure 3.1 provides a sample of what one approach might look like for schools that use a standardized protocol for Tier 2 instruction and a problem-solving protocol for Tier 3. For schools using a problem-solving model for Tier 2 instruction, then it would be necessary to use the diagnostic assessments that we describe in Tier 3 during Tier 2.

	Tier 1	Tier 2	Tier 3 and Special Education
	General education with differentiation	3–5×/week 30–45 minutes Small group (3–6 homogeneous) Standard protocol	5×/week 45 minutes Individual or pair with common needs Problem-solving protocol
Screening 3×/year	Prescribed CBMs		Any off-grade-level screening measures (determined from a history of working with a small subset of students)
	Text level—Benchmark Running record (K–2) or grade-level informal reading inventory Informal screening measures		
Diagnostic: tests selected for particular children based on screening results	Phonological awareness tasks (K–1) Informal phonics inventory (grades 1–2)	Program—prescribed	Phonological awareness tasks Detailed phonics inventory Textbook interview Metacognitive/strategy interview Attitude survey
Progress monitoring	*Monthly—students performing below level* Text level (K–2) High-frequency words (K–3) Oral reading fluency (grades 2–6)	*Every 2 weeks* CBMs specific to targeted intervention	*Every week* CBMs specific to targeted skills (with grade-level adjustments, as needed) Text reading level (K–2) High-frequency word inventories (as needed in grades 3–4) Retelling idea units (as needed in grades 3–6)
Other	State-mandated tests Program criterion-referenced tests	Program criterion-referenced tests	*(Optional)* Woodcock–Johnson Achievement Battery Peabody Picture Vocabulary Test–IV Expressive Vocabulary Test–2

FIGURE 3.1. Sample assessment system summary for a three-tiered framework.

Our model is based on the premise that *all* students are receiving a comprehensive literacy program in Tier 1 *and* differentiated literacy instruction in Tier 1. Students who have demonstrated risk factors for one or two components of reading instruction are receiving an intense standardized intervention in that area for 30–45 minutes 3–5 days a week in a Tier 2 setting.

Students who have been identified as extremely at risk, either by very low achievement scores on multiple assessments or lack of progress in Tier 2, are placed in Tier 3 settings that apply a problem-solving model in which deep diagnostics are used to target individual strengths and weaknesses. A reading expert provides research-based instruction (*not* a one-size-fits-all program) individually or in groups of no more than three children with similar needs. In the event that children do not make progress or seem to require this level of sustained support to make progress, normed, standardized tests that enable statistically reliable comparisons to other children in their age group are administered by the Tier 3 teacher before beginning a referral process.

Nurture and Fertilize

Typically, nurturing and fertilizing will most heavily involve professional development about the assessments that teachers have committed to performing. The fifth column of the assessment audit provides a means of indicating the type of professional development needed for each assessment. Often, schools conduct a one-shot session once an assessment has been selected, but thorough, formal professional development is needed to ensure that all teachers are administering and scoring the assessments in a standardized way. More difficult is the translation of assessment scores into instructional practices. Doing so requires the sustained in-class professional development and follow-up provided by a coach or lesson study with peer observations. Principals are key players in establishing these infrastructures. Additionally, several schools may need to pool their resources to provide specialized training in particular assessments such as the TOWRE, C-TOPP, and WJ III NU ACH for Tier 3 teachers, special educators, and school psychologists. This approach avoids the assumption that universities have provided adequate training for specialized faculty in current assessment practices.

The same is true for adding a fidelity component and booster sessions. In order for RTI to work, the data must be trustworthy. Providing some infrastructure that allows peers to conduct a periodic fidelity check on each other increases the likelihood that both teachers adhere more closely to the standardized testing procedures. It is important that this be done in an educational rather than evaluative manner so that both parties understand that the object is to learn something from the process. Therefore, it is not a good idea to designate one faculty team (e.g., special education teachers or Reading Recovery teachers) as the more knowledgeable others who are sent in to judge whether classroom teachers are "following the rules." Ideally, if schedules allow it, two knowledgeable peers might conduct the occasional fidelity checks in a reciprocal manner thus refining and nurturing their own knowledge about the assessment procedures.

Nurturing the assessment system in a deliberate and sustained way saves time and money for a school when taking the long view. Creating a system that provides reliable data from year to year, from teacher to teacher, will result in the administration of fewer tests. Tests are administered more quickly and accurately. As a result, the instruction will be more finely targeted to students' needs so that achievement can be maximized.

FORM 3.1

The RTI Assessment Audit

A comprehensive assessment system will involve multiple and varied types of evaluative tools designed to provide information that guides and informs instruction. The RTI Assessment Audit is a review of assessment practices implemented by a school in the area of literacy across grade levels. Conducting the RTI Assessment Audit serves several purposes:

1. Identifies the different types of assessments used in the area of literacy;
2. Clarifies the purpose (screening, progress monitoring, diagnostic, and outcome) of each assessment tool;
3. Identifies the construct being assessed (e.g., concepts of print, comprehension, fluency);
4. Identifies training needs of staff members relative to the administration and interpretation of targeted assessments; and
5. Provides an opportunity for a school to identify redundancies or gaps in the assessment process.

Directions: For each grade level, identify:

1. **Name of the assessment tool** (Include full name of tool administered.)
2. **Primary purpose** (Check the box next to the primary purpose for each tool listed.)
3. **Construct assessed** (Check the box[es] that indicate what specific literacy element or area is being evaluated.)
4. **Frequency of administration** (For each tool identify the number of times it is administered each year.)
5. **Staff training required** (Identify the level of training that has been conducted.)
6. **Redundancies** (List any assessments that duplicate the information obtained from another tool.)
7. **Voids** (Identify gaps in assessment information.)

(cont.)

The RTI Assessment Audit *(page 2 of 10)*

Purpose	Description	Examples
Screening	Brief assessments designed to provide preliminary indication of which students may be at risk for reading difficulties.	Phoneme Segmentation Fluency Dynamic Indicators of Basic Early Literacy Skills (DIBELS) AIMSweb Tests Informal Reading Inventories or Kits to determine instructional reading level
Diagnostic	Individually administered assessments used for the purposes of gaining a more precise picture of students' skills and knowledge. Information obtained is used to plan instruction.	Discrete Phonemic Awareness Tasks Informal Phonics Inventory Informal Reading Inventory (comprehension sections/think-alouds)
Progress monitoring	Brief assessment typically administered for the purposes of determining if a student is making adequate progress.	Dynamic Indicators of Basic Early Literacy Skills (DIBELS)—Oral Reading Fluency
Outcome	Assessments that are commonly administered on a group basis at the end of the year. Primarily used to determine if particular instructional or policy goals are being met, though they may also be used to examine trends in learning.	State English Language Arts Assessment—Grade 3

The RTI Assessment Audit (page 3 of 10)

Grade	Assessment Tool	Tester	Construct Assessed											Function	Training
			Concepts of Print	Phonological Awareness	Word Recognition Decoding/High Freq.	Spelling Development	Reading Fluency	Conceptual Vocabulary	Comprehension	Writing Process	Motivation/Attitudes	Other			
KINDERGARTEN														☐Screening ☐Diagnostic ☐Progress Monitoring ☐Outcome	☐Introduction ☐Fidelity Checks ☐Regular Boosters
														☐Screening ☐Diagnostic ☐Progress Monitoring ☐Outcome	☐Introduction ☐Fidelity Checks ☐Regular Boosters
														☐Screening ☐Diagnostic ☐Progress Monitoring ☐Outcome	☐Introduction ☐Fidelity Checks ☐Regular Boosters
														☐Screening ☐Diagnostic ☐Progress Monitoring ☐Outcome	☐Introduction ☐Fidelity Checks ☐Regular Boosters
														☐Screening ☐Diagnostic ☐Progress Monitoring ☐Outcome	☐Introduction ☐Fidelity Checks ☐Regular Boosters
														☐Screening ☐Diagnostic ☐Progress Monitoring ☐Outcome	☐Introduction ☐Fidelity Checks ☐Regular Boosters

The RTI Assessment Audit *(page 4 of 10)*

Grade	Assessment Tool	Tester	Concepts of Print	Phonological Awareness	Word Recognition Decoding/High Freq.	Spelling Development	Reading Fluency	Conceptual Vocabulary	Comprehension	Writing Process	Motivation/ Attitudes	Other	Function	Training
													☐Screening ☐Diagnostic ☐Progress Monitoring ☐Outcome	☐Introduction ☐Fidelity Checks ☐Regular Boosters
													☐Screening ☐Diagnostic ☐Progress Monitoring ☐Outcome	☐Introduction ☐Fidelity Checks ☐Regular Boosters
FIRST GRADE													☐Screening ☐Diagnostic ☐Progress Monitoring ☐Outcome	☐Introduction ☐Fidelity Checks ☐Regular Boosters
													☐Screening ☐Diagnostic ☐Progress Monitoring ☐Outcome	☐Introduction ☐Fidelity Checks ☐Regular Boosters
													☐Screening ☐Diagnostic ☐Progress Monitoring ☐Outcome	☐Introduction ☐Fidelity Checks ☐Regular Boosters
													☐Screening ☐Diagnostic ☐Progress Monitoring ☐Outcome	☐Introduction ☐Fidelity Checks ☐Regular Boosters

(Construct Assessed spans: Concepts of Print, Phonological Awareness, Word Recognition Decoding/High Freq., Spelling Development, Reading Fluency, Conceptual Vocabulary, Comprehension, Writing Process, Motivation/Attitudes, Other)

The RTI Assessment Audit *(page 5 of 10)*

Grade	Assessment Tool	Tester	Construct Assessed											Function	Training
			Concepts of Print	Phonological Awareness	Word Recognition Decoding/High Freq.	Spelling Development	Reading Fluency	Conceptual Vocabulary	Comprehension	Writing Process	Motivation/ Attitudes	Other			
SECOND GRADE														☐Screening ☐Diagnostic ☐Progress Monitoring ☐Outcome	☐Introduction ☐Fidelity Checks ☐Regular Boosters
														☐Screening ☐Diagnostic ☐Progress Monitoring ☐Outcome	☐Introduction ☐Fidelity Checks ☐Regular Boosters
														☐Screening ☐Diagnostic ☐Progress Monitoring ☐Outcome	☐Introduction ☐Fidelity Checks ☐Regular Boosters
														☐Screening ☐Diagnostic ☐Progress Monitoring ☐Outcome	☐Introduction ☐Fidelity Checks ☐Regular Boosters
														☐Screening ☐Diagnostic ☐Progress Monitoring ☐Outcome	☐Introduction ☐Fidelity Checks ☐Regular Boosters
														☐Screening ☐Diagnostic ☐Progress Monitoring ☐Outcome	☐Introduction ☐Fidelity Checks ☐Regular Boosters

The RTI Assessment Audit *(page 6 of 10)*

Grade	Assessment Tool	Tester	Construct Assessed												Function	Training
			Concepts of Print	Phonological Awareness	Word Recognition Decoding/High Freq.	Spelling Development	Reading Fluency	Conceptual Vocabulary	Comprehension	Writing Process	Motivation/ Attitudes	Other				
THIRD GRADE														☐Screening ☐Diagnostic ☐Progress Monitoring ☐Outcome	☐Introduction ☐Fidelity Checks ☐Regular Boosters
														☐Screening ☐Diagnostic ☐Progress Monitoring ☐Outcome	☐Introduction ☐Fidelity Checks ☐Regular Boosters
														☐Screening ☐Diagnostic ☐Progress Monitoring ☐Outcome	☐Introduction ☐Fidelity Checks ☐Regular Boosters
														☐Screening ☐Diagnostic ☐Progress Monitoring ☐Outcome	☐Introduction ☐Fidelity Checks ☐Regular Boosters
														☐Screening ☐Diagnostic ☐Progress Monitoring ☐Outcome	☐Introduction ☐Fidelity Checks ☐Regular Boosters
														☐Screening ☐Diagnostic ☐Progress Monitoring ☐Outcome	☐Introduction ☐Fidelity Checks ☐Regular Boosters

The RTI Assessment Audit *(page 7 of 10)*

Grade	Assessment Tool	Tester	Construct Assessed											Function	Training
			Concepts of Print	Phonological Awareness	Word Recognition Decoding/High Freq.	Spelling Development	Reading Fluency	Conceptual Vocabulary	Comprehension	Writing Process	Motivation/ Attitudes	Other		
FOURTH GRADE														☐ Screening ☐ Diagnostic ☐ Progress Monitoring ☐ Outcome	☐ Introduction ☐ Fidelity Checks ☐ Regular Boosters
													☐ Screening ☐ Diagnostic ☐ Progress Monitoring ☐ Outcome	☐ Introduction ☐ Fidelity Checks ☐ Regular Boosters
													☐ Screening ☐ Diagnostic ☐ Progress Monitoring ☐ Outcome	☐ Introduction ☐ Fidelity Checks ☐ Regular Boosters
													☐ Screening ☐ Diagnostic ☐ Progress Monitoring ☐ Outcome	☐ Introduction ☐ Fidelity Checks ☐ Regular Boosters
													☐ Screening ☐ Diagnostic ☐ Progress Monitoring ☐ Outcome	☐ Introduction ☐ Fidelity Checks ☐ Regular Boosters
													☐ Screening ☐ Diagnostic ☐ Progress Monitoring ☐ Outcome	☐ Introduction ☐ Fidelity Checks ☐ Regular Boosters

The RTI Assessment Audit *(page 8 of 10)*

Grade	Assessment Tool	Tester	Construct Assessed											Function	Training
			Concepts of Print	Phonological Awareness	Word Recognition Decoding/High Freq.	Spelling Development	Reading Fluency	Conceptual Vocabulary	Comprehension	Writing Process	Motivation/ Attitudes	Other			
FIFTH GRADE														☐Screening ☐Diagnostic ☐Progress Monitoring ☐Outcome	☐Introduction ☐Fidelity Checks ☐Regular Boosters
														☐Screening ☐Diagnostic ☐Progress Monitoring ☐Outcome	☐Introduction ☐Fidelity Checks ☐Regular Boosters
														☐Screening ☐Diagnostic ☐Progress Monitoring ☐Outcome	☐Introduction ☐Fidelity Checks ☐Regular Boosters
														☐Screening ☐Diagnostic ☐Progress Monitoring ☐Outcome	☐Introduction ☐Fidelity Checks ☐Regular Boosters
														☐Screening ☐Diagnostic ☐Progress Monitoring ☐Outcome	☐Introduction ☐Fidelity Checks ☐Regular Boosters
														☐Screening ☐Diagnostic ☐Progress Monitoring ☐Outcome	☐Introduction ☐Fidelity Checks ☐Regular Boosters
														☐Screening ☐Diagnostic ☐Progress Monitoring ☐Outcome	☐Introduction ☐Fidelity Checks ☐Regular Boosters

The RTI Assessment Audit *(page 9 of 10)*

REDUNDANCIES

Grade	Are there any redundancies?	Identify
K	☐ Yes ☐ No	
1	☐ Yes ☐ No	
2	☐ Yes ☐ No	
3	☐ Yes ☐ No	
4	☐ Yes ☐ No	
5	☐ Yes ☐ No	

The RTI Assessment Audit *(page 10 of 10)*

| Grade | Are there any voids? | VOIDS |
		Identify
K	☐ Yes ☐ No	
1	☐ Yes ☐ No	
2	☐ Yes ☐ No	
3	☐ Yes ☐ No	
4	☐ Yes ☐ No	
5	☐ Yes ☐ No	

CHAPTER FOUR

Assessments in Tier 1

The Essentials

A s we have discussed, RTI employs a multi-tiered progressive system of increasingly intense levels of instruction. Tier 1 literacy instruction is the least intensive and most comprehensive tier and is offered universally to all students. It is provided by the general education instructor in the regular classroom. One of the foundational tenets of RTI is that Tier 1 consists of competent teachers providing evidence-based literacy instruction to all students. High-quality Tier 1 serves as the first defense against inadequate achievement. Competent teachers who engage in ongoing professional development apply teaching strategies and materials that have been shown to yield achievement gains with similar types of students (Wixson, Lipson, & Johnston, 2010). Even when research-based instruction is provided, however, success is not guaranteed. Not all students will respond in the same way. Therefore, within Tier 1 there must be the time, flexibility, and resources to provide differentiated instruction (Walpole & McKenna, 2007). Differentiation addresses academic, linguistic, and cultural variation as indicated by observation and assessment. Tier 1 assessments provide a general overview of whether children are functioning above level, on level, approaching level, or below level. Additionally, they provide developmental indicators of student mastery and an instructional map for future directions.

Generally, the classroom teacher, with occasional assistance from the Tier 2 teacher or literacy coach, will administer the set of assessments described below to inform Tier 1 instruction. Due to the importance and comprehensiveness of the classroom literacy program, the classroom teacher bears the heaviest burden for literacy assessment. Some schools prefer to employ a SWAT-team approach, assigning a small team of trained specialists to do the majority of testing. While this approach might increase the likelihood of fidelity to standardized testing procedures, we find that the results are not as meaningful to teachers when others have collected the data. Table 4.1 provides a summary of the assessments that are useful for informing Tier 1 instruction and that are likely to be administered by the Tier 1 teacher. If a SWAT team is employed, it makes the most sense for them to administer the CBMs that serve as a gauge of reading wellness (screening measures), but that are not as useful for informing instruction (diagnostics). We believe that when classroom

TABLE 4.1. Assessments to Inform Tier 1 Instruction

Type of assessment	Test	Administration	Frequency Recipients
Screening	CBM prescribed by grade level and school	Individual	3×/year Everyone
Informal screening measures	Text level—Benchmark	Individual	3×/year
	Running record (K–2) or grade-level informal reading inventory (grades 3–5)		Everyone
	Elementary spelling inventory (grades 1–5)	Whole class or small group	3×/year Everyone
	Writing samples (grades 1–5)	Whole class	3×/year Everyone
	High-frequency word list (grades K–3)	Individual	3×/year until mastery Everyone
	Letter identification (K–early 1)	Individual	Monthly until mastery Everyone
	Hearing sounds in words (Clay, 2006; McKenna & Stahl, 2009) (K–early 1)	Small group or individual	K—midyear/end of year 1—beginning of year Everyone
	Contemporary vocabulary (K. A. D. Stahl & Bravo, 2010) (grades 2–5)	Whole group	Pre- and postcontent units Everyone
Diagnostics for a few particular children as indicated by other assessments	Phonological awareness tasks (K–1)	Individual	As needed
	Informal phonics inventory (grades 1–2)	Individual	As needed
	Z-Test (McKenna & Stahl, 2009) (grades 1–2)	Individual	As needed
Progress monitoring (children performing below level only)	Text level (K–2)	Individual	Monthly (low performers)
	High-frequency words (K–3)	Individual	Monthly (low performers)
	Oral reading fluency (grades 2–5)	Individual	Monthly (low fluency, not in Tier 2)

teachers give diagnostic assessments, there is likely to be a higher level of reflection and buy-in.

SCREENING ASSESSMENT

Curriculum-Based Measures

The selected CBMs used for screening should be administered three times a year. Schools that choose to screen four times a year need to carefully weigh the benefits of additional test data in relationship to lost instructional time. In the lower grades, CBM screening requires individual administration. While many advocates of these tasks minimize the strain of giving a 1-minute task to each child, any teacher who has been required to give these tests knows that they aren't really 1-minute measures. Usually there is a set of measures or repeated measures that require at least 5 to 10 minutes per child. Teachers are typically challenged to constructively occupy and manage the other students while administering the tests. Approximately 4 hours will need to be allocated to the administration of the DIBELS Next ORF subtest with retelling follow-up for a class of 25 students. In the beginning of the year, before Tier 2 groups are operational, the Tier 2 teacher may share this task with the classroom teacher whose students he or she will be supporting. In the upper grades, the screening burden is lighter. For example, the maze can quickly be administered in either a whole-class or small-group setting.

Establishing an Instructional Reading Level

It is imperative for the classroom teacher to collect a sample of connected text reading that mirrors the kind of reading that the students will be expected to do as part of their daily literacy and content-area instruction. In the primary grades, this sample would be likely to consist of a running record of each student's oral reading of text that has been leveled using a fine gradient of difficulty (Fountas & Pinnell, 2006, 2010; Peterson, 1991). We caution, however, against the assumption that leveling represents a precise measure of text difficulty. Passages corresponding to text reading levels have been shown to vary considerably (Hiebert & Pearson, 2010), and care should be taken to view the results as approximations only—as estimates that may be trumped by other data.

Once samples of oral reading have been acquired, miscue analysis can provide insights regarding the appropriate instructional level and the novice reader's ability to orchestrate decoding and making sense of text simultaneously. Again, we need to sound a note of caution. Miscue analysis is useful principally as a way of detecting a student's growth toward code-based word recognition (McKenna & Picard, 2006/2007). Originally, miscue analysis was a way to ensure that students were using context to predict words. For example, saying "pony" for *horse*, and other "semantically acceptable" substitutions, were viewed as signs a student was constructing meaning. This idea has since been discarded because it is based on a flawed model of the reading process (Stanovich, 1980, 2000). Although it is true that children often use context to make such substitutions, they do so in order to compensate for weak decoding skills. Miscue analysis is still viable, but semantically acceptable miscues should not be viewed as a sign of proficiency but as an indication that more work in decoding is needed.

Finally, the use of a retelling scale and prosodic rating scale provides a gauge of comprehension and prosody at the child's specific instructional reading level. Although prosody and retelling are generally correlated, exceptions can be revealing. As an adult you well recall an instance when you were asked to read a selection "cold" to a group of peers. If your experiences have been similar to ours, your attention may have been directed principally at a good oral rendition (so as not to embarrass yourself). When you finished, you may have hoped secretly that no one asked you any questions about the content. Children often face a similar dilemma when asked to read aloud, especially in the upper grades, and it is not unusual for good oral reading to be accompanied by disappointing comprehension. The reverse can occur too, when the child is intent on comprehending and makes sacrifices in prosody. Disagreements between prosody and retelling can be resolved by gathering additional data in multiple settings in order to determine the cause and possible remediation for the discrepancy.

In third grade and beyond, it is likely that records from the primary grades enable a text-level approximation. Students whose records indicate that they are functioning on grade level or above grade level should silently read material from an informal reading inventory (Johns, 2011; Leslie & Caldwell, 2010) or some other inventory assessment kit such as the Developmental Reading Assessment (Beaver, 1997) or Fountas and Pinnell's Benchmark Assessment System (2010). Only students who are new to the school or who are reading with an instructional reading level at or below second grade should be reading the passages orally. Beyond second grade level, the focus is on comprehension. So the retelling and ability to answer a range of questions dominates the determination of the instructional level.

Assessing comprehension based on graded passages may sound like a tedious, time-consuming process. As a result, many schools have forsaken it and have embraced the exclusive use of CBMs. They may be using the Lexiles (Stenner, Burdick, Sanford, & Burdick, 2007) that are statistically derived from AIMSweb reports or using WCPM benchmarks to assign instructional levels. These shortcuts compromise the very diagnostic information provided by inventories that is most useful for targeting specific kinds of instruction needed by children reading either above or below grade level (Valencia et al., 2010). In other words, the CBMs can tell you who is behind (most teachers knew that before administering the CBMs) but they cannot inform teachers about where reading development is suffering and what is needed to remedy it. They do not provide any indicator that the proficient reader can provide a comprehensive retelling, but is really unable to critically evaluate a text or identify a character's motives. Teachers need this information to plan instruction that will enable their students to become more proficient readers and to meet the demands of the Common Core Standards.

There are some ways to make this process more time efficient. In the primary grades, running records can be collected during small-group instruction. In the beginning of the year, before instructional levels have been determined, testing can occur within the teacher-led group as part of the class orientation to the small-group time routine.

In the intermediate and upper grades, the children are more independent so there is more flexibility. Silent reading can occur in a small-group setting, immediately followed by the teacher asking individual students to retell and answer questions. Additionally, if children have been in the school for the previous year, there should be an existing record of the approximate instructional reading level. Therefore, the screening test typically requires application of only one narrative and one informational passage for determining the instructional level. The goal in Tier 1 is to determine the instructional reading level using the assessment passage and to estimate the independent text level and frustration level based on more informal observations and data collection during instruction. Those students who are below level may present more complicated profiles and require a series of off-level tests. These should be administered by the Tier 2 or Tier 3 teacher. The benefit of this approach is that the classroom teacher is able to administer fewer reading passages to greater numbers of students. On the other hand, the Tier 2 and Tier 3 teachers will be testing fewer students, and they might consequently have time to administer a wider range of off-grade-level passages.

Once a school attains fidelity to assessment practices and a consistent system is in place, this process of determining instructional reading levels occurs fairly quickly within the first 2 or 3 weeks of the school year. However, when results are unreliable from one grade level or one class to the next, the process is time consuming because the prepared passages are either too easy or too hard for the children and multiple texts need to be administered to each child. Lack of reliability of test results from classroom to classroom drains instructional time and, worse, can cause it to be used in nonproductive ways. Therefore, it is worth devoting time to training sessions, assessment boosters, and test-fidelity checks to make the assessment process itself more reliable and time efficient.

CBMs, writing samples, and isolated reading skill tests, such as word lists and spelling inventories, should be completed first to get children back up to speed after a summer reprieve that often causes a reading-level dip. However, waiting more than 2 weeks into the new school year to conduct reading assessments in order to begin instructional-level and skills-based reading groups simply aggravates the situation. An assertive instructional program in September (or August in many communities) is the best medicine for summer vacation lapses. Easing back into instruction only delays and compromises the achievement needed by those who did the least during the summer, thus contributing to the achievement gap.

Group-Administered Informal Assessments

Typically when one thinks of screening assessments, CBMs come to mind. However, there are some other informal assessments that conscientious general education teachers use as both screening tools and to inform instruction. A spelling inventory (Bear et al., 2011; Ganske, 2000; McKenna & Stahl, 2009) and a writing sample can both be administered in a whole-group setting. The spelling inventory takes about 10 minutes and the writing sample varies from 20 to 45 minutes, depending on the grade level of the students. Writing samples based on a common grade-level prompt are typically collected during one writing workshop period or during a portion of a general literacy block. Both the spelling inventory and writing sample provide a treasure trove of instructional directives. Spelling inventories are scored using a feature guide that pinpoints instructional needs, and writing samples are scored using a commonly agreed-upon rubric such as the 6 + 1 Writing Trait® Rubric (*http://educationnorthwest.org/resource/464*). It's hard to find more informative measures for such minimal time investment.

First, you can use a developmental spelling inventory to structure your entire word study curriculum in a differentiated manner. Or if your school has chosen a particular word-study curriculum, you can use the qualitative information to ensure that the curriculum materials are targeted to the appropriate developmental skill areas for the students, especially those functioning far above or below level. Second, the quantitative scoring system can be used to trace the growth of children, classrooms, and grade levels over time for program evaluation purposes. Because most core programs and commercial phonics programs apply criterion measures, the spelling inventory can serve as a form of transfer outcome-based measure to evaluate commercial program application. Regardless of what spelling program a school chooses, children grow along a predictable trajectory of awareness but at different rates. The spelling inventory can provide information that will allow you to determine whether your commercial spelling program is equally effective for children at different points on the developmental continuum.

Foundational Skills

In kindergarten and grade 1, the classroom teacher will also want to conduct some individually administered tests, such as those that assess letter names and high-frequency words (see Table 4.1). Because these two skills are so important, teachers need to know precisely which letters and words are recognized automatically and which ones need to be explicitly taught and practiced by the children in their class. A CBM such as the DIBELS Next Letter Naming Fluency subtest can provide a quick indication of whether a problem exists. However, its random presentation of letters is not designed to be diagnostic. Simply knowing that a kindergartner can name 28 letters in 1 minute is not enough. If a CBM identifies a problem, the proper follow-up is an alphabet inventory, such as the one developed by McKenna and Stahl (2009, p. 97). Automatic recognition of the most common high-frequency words is likewise of key importance. Teachers who suspect that a child cannot recognize those words expected at their grade level can administer a high-frequency word inventory, such as one based on the Dolch words (see McKenna & Stahl, 2009, pp. 123–124) or on the Fry Instant Words (McKenna & Stahl, 2009, pp. 116–122). These diagnostic inventories can become the basis of a tracking system to monitor the progress of individual children as high-frequency words are taught and practiced over time.

During the small-group instruction, the teacher needs to target instruction to particular letters and high-frequency words that these inventories have indicated were unknown by particular children. Readministering these criterion measures on a monthly basis enables teachers to keep a close eye on the ongoing growth of foundational skills with specificity of child and skill in mind. This kind of differentiated instruction and accountability needs to take place before one can identify that a child is in need of a second tier of instruction. Too often a screening CBM is administered, an instructional program is then applied with fidelity in a general way to all children, and a screening CBM is later readministered. The frequent result is that, despite the program, particular children still appear to be in high-risk (or low-percentile) categories compared to their grade cohort. It is tempting to conclude that they have not responded to the intervention. However, between the two tests the instruction was never personalized during differentiated classroom instruction to ensure mastery of the discrete list of items that they needed to learn.

We offer one final bit of advice concerning assessments that target a systematized list of letter names and high-frequency words. There is a curious fact that makes these tests exempt from our usual caution about overtesting. Consider Bill, whose teacher is administering the Dolch inventory. On being shown the word *about*, Bill cannot produce its pronunciation. Rather than silently recording this fact and moving on to the next word, Bill's teacher says the word and has Bill repeat it before moving on. This is not a case of teaching to the test. Providing feedback about words and letters is fair game on inventories like these. This is because the words and letters on the inventories are the entire curriculum. They are not a sample of a larger curriculum. On a vocabulary test like the PPVT, it would be entirely inappropriate to provide feedback about individual words. This is because the words included are intended to represent a much larger universe of word meanings. Teaching just those words would defeat the idea of sampling and would yield an inflated estimate of vocabulary knowledge. But in the case of high-frequency words and letter names, the inventories comprise exactly the items to be taught. Providing feedback during instruction is a way of combining assessment and instruction.

Conceptual Vocabulary

At the onset of each content-area unit, some determination needs to be made regarding the students' level of knowledge of the disciplinary vocabulary. During a school's assessment audit, the faculty will need to decide how they wish to approach this task. Typically, grade-level teams decide on a list of target vocabulary for each state-mandated science and social studies unit for that grade level. Then a vocabulary pre- and posttest can be constructed for each unit to determine the level of vocabulary growth that occurred during the unit. These tests might take the form of the traditional matching, multiple-choice, or cloze tasks that are found in most textbooks. The Vocabulary Recognition Task, the Vocabulary Assessment Magazine, and vocabulary knowledge scales are more contemporary measures that are sensitive enough to reflect incremental growth and depth of word knowledge within a content unit as opposed to simply measuring breadth of knowledge (see K. A. D. Stahl & Bravo, 2010). Additionally, they possess characteristics that make them appropriate and useful with both English-only students and English learners. Teams of teachers who undertake the construction of these forms of vocabulary assessment report more deliberate instructional attention to conceptual development during the units.

These pre- and post-teacher-constructed assessments are primarily intended to serve the progress monitoring function. The words included on such a test are likely to be unfamiliar to the children. After all, the point of the unit is to introduce these concepts. Moreover, the pretest does not operate as a screening test. Even if some of the children know some of the words, they will not be exempted from the unit, which is likely to deepen and reinforce their conceptual understanding. Nor does it serve as a diagnostic test, which would reveal the exact words to teach. Because disciplinary words are generally taught in related clusters, it would make no sense to try to separate those that may be known in advance to some students. In addition, the number of exposures needed to acquire deep word understanding is typically more than 12 (S. A. Stahl & Nagy, 2006), and so it makes little difference whether the unit is a word's first exposure for one student and the fifth for another. Both students will benefit.

Rather, our primary concern is whether our instructional approaches lead to acceptable growth in knowledge of the words we target. Pre- and postassessments can provide answers to this question. It is for this reason that they are consistent with the underlying idea of RTI, and when we find that children are not learning the words we target, our first reaction should be to record which methods we used and to systematically try other research-based methods.

DIAGNOSTICS

We hold these truths to be self-evident: Diagnostic assessment at Tier 1 should not be complicated or time consuming, its results should be easy to interpret and implement, and it should be aimed at foundational skills.

Remember that a diagnostic test informs instruction by suggesting a specific focus. Where foundational skills are concerned, the cognitive model begins with fluency from the middle of first grade to the end of elementary school. For children below the fluency benchmark, screening in decoding is conducted. If performance is below the benchmark, screening in phonological awareness is undertaken. At the point where problems arise, diagnostic testing is used to determine instructional targets.

Figure 4.1 presents this strategy as a decision tree. It is similar to the generic assessment strategy in Figure 1.2 in Chapter 1, but it is specific to fluency and identifies the diagnostic assessments needed. It should be clear at once that diagnostic assessments work in tandem with screening instruments and that diagnostics are a last resort.

Let's follow the logic of the diagnostic strategy with Laura, a second grader. We will use DIBELS Next measures for convenience. If Laura's ORF score is at or above benchmark, she is not tested any further. Walpole and McKenna (2007, 2009) recommend that small-group differentiated instruction focus on vocabulary and comprehension. But what happens if Laura's score falls below the benchmark? It may be tempting to provide instruction in fluency—after all, she has fallen short of the fluency benchmark—but the cognitive model indicates that more basic problems be ruled out first. We would next screen in decoding, giving the DIBELS Next NWF subtest. If her performance on this measure is at benchmark, we would indeed provide instruction in fluency. If, on the other hand, she is below benchmark on the decoding screening test (NWF), we might be inclined to give a diagnostic in this area, such as a decoding inventory. Once again, however, the cognitive model cautions us first to rule out phonological awareness as a root problem. If Laura's score on a phonological awareness screening measure, such as the DIBELS Next Phoneme Segmentation (PSF) subtest, is at benchmark, we should then administer a decoding inventory and also evaluate her high-frequency word inventory to identify instructional targets. If, however, Laura falls below the benchmark on PSF, a diagnostic would be required, such as the Tests of Phonemic Awareness (McKenna & Stahl, 2009, p. 98), which would present Laura with a progression of short tasks culminating in phoneme segmentation.

Note that this system requires just two diagnostic assessments: inventories in decoding and phonological awareness. There are several choices of which inventories to use, but one of each should be in every teacher's assessment toolkit. We strongly recommend that these assessments be mutually agreed on so that consistent records can be kept and meaningful conversations about a child's progress can occur among teachers. Although these inventories can and should become mainstays in an RTI system, we remind you that diagnostic information can also be gleaned from the other sources we have discussed, such as running records and retellings.

A final point concerns children in kindergarten and the first half of grade 1. Because fluency benchmarks do not exist before the middle of grade 1, the strategy in Figure 4.1 must be simplified. We can do this by beginning at the second level and asking first whether the child is at benchmark in decoding and then following the remainder of the strategy.

PROGRESS MONITORING

Most educators would agree that teachers are constantly monitoring the ongoing progress of their students. However, this term has become more prevalent in the era of RTI. Typically, within an RTI framework *progress monitoring* is the label applied to the periodic assessments used to determine how well a child is responding to a particular intervention. The administration of progress monitoring assessments increases in frequency as the intensity of the intervention increases. Therefore, the progress monitoring tasks are administered less frequently in Tier 1 than in either

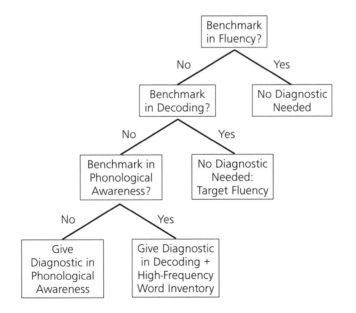

FIGURE 4.1. Assessment strategy for foundational skills.

Tier 2 or Tier 3. In Tier 1, most progress monitoring tasks might only be administered monthly to a subset of students. To put this idea another way, the frequency of administration should correlate with the level of concern. Progress monitoring tasks should be matched with the student's area of need. Children who have recently been discontinued from Tier 2 or Tier 3 instruction need to receive more frequent progress monitoring than children who have consistently functioned successfully without supplementary support. Classroom teachers should also increase the frequency of progress monitoring for a child who displays an erratic assessment profile or erratic performance on a particular task.

Tijuana, a first-grade EL student, began the school year scoring low in all areas that were screened. Her instructional text level was Fountas and Pinnell Level B. On DIBELS Next she scored in the 42nd percentile rank in letter identification, but she placed below the 25th percentile rank on NWF and below the 10th percentile rank on PSF (Cummings, Kennedy, Otterstedt, Baker, & Kame'enui, 2011). In addition to the general comprehensive literacy curriculum, she received classroom-differentiated small-group instruction at her instructional reading level and at her developmental word-study level (early letter name—short vowels). She also was placed in a Tier 2 standard protocol intervention using a commercial phonics program. By the midyear screening, she was functioning above the 50th percentile rank on the DIBELS Next measures of NWF and PSF. Tier 2 progress monitoring scores in these areas had consistently reflected a positive trajectory with scores on nonsense words and phoneme segmentation consistently above her aim line. However, despite the improved phonics scores, her instructional text reading level was only a Level D, still considerably below the grade-level expectation of Level F. Not surprisingly, her ORF WCPM was 16, placing her in the 24th percentile rank (Cummings et al., 2011). Due to financial limitations, this school's only first-grade Tier 2 intervention was the standardized phonics program. The data for this EL student do not present a need for intensive, small-group phonics instruction any longer. She needs support and coaching in applying sophisticated decoding strategies on the run during reading connected text. The data team (including her classroom teacher, Tier 2 teacher, literacy coach, and assistant principal in charge of curriculum) recommended increased attention to mastery of high-frequency words and ensuring that instructional-level guided reading was conducted in a small homogeneous group 5 days a week. Classroom progress monitoring included biweekly running records and miscue analysis to inform instruction with biweekly high-frequency-word-CBM progress monitoring on alternate weeks.

Why not provide Tier 2 support? Her test scores did not indicate a need for more small-group intense phonics instruction, the focus of her school's first-grade secondary intervention. Based on her EL status and her challenges reading connected text, the data team determined that she needed concentrated practice reading high volumes of connected text and follow-up discussion. This could best be provided within the differentiated instruction provided in the classroom, not the Tier 2 phonics curriculum.

Text Level (K–2)

In the early school years (kindergarten through early second grade), the utilization of a fine text gradient is essential for sensitive measurement of connected text reading growth (Hiebert & Pearson, 2010). Schools may choose from many alternatives, such as Fountas and Pinnell (2006, 2010; see Table 4.2), Peterson (1991), the Developmental Reading Assessment (Beaver), or Lexiles. Reading development proceeds rapidly along several fronts during this time. A child's knowledge of how words and books work expands, as does an understanding of the alphabetic–phonetic system. At the same time, the number of high-frequency words the child can automatically retrieve continues to grow. Consequently, monitoring children's progression of successful reading of increasingly difficult texts is among the most important assessments because it reveals how well the child can integrate various skill sets while reading. We stress that monitoring progress in this way is not a substitute for keeping up with specific skill acquisition. It can, however, open a different window on reading development and shed light on how well a child can orchestrate the use of these skills during reading. Although weighing a pig doesn't make it fatter, a visual representation of where children are and the growth pattern can increase a teacher's awareness and sense of urgency for instructional intervention. A text-level progress monitoring chart (see Form 4.1 at the end of the chapter) that reflects the same level for three consecutive data points (3 months) in the primary grades should shout out to the Tier 1 teacher that a student's instruction needs modification. Form 4.2 (at the end of the chapter) might be used in the upper grades for children in Tier 2 and Tier 3.

Because the running record of early reading provides so much diagnostic information, it not only serves as the scale telling us where the child is but the miscue

TABLE 4.2. Progress Monitoring Chart for Instructional Text Reading Levels

Grade	Months of the school year									
	1	2	3	4	5	6	7	8	9	10
K			A	B	B	C	C	C/D	D	D
1	D/E	E	F/G	G	H	H	I	I	J	J
2	J/K	K	K	K	L	L	L	M	M	M
3	M/N	N	N	N	O	O	O	P	P	P
4	P/Q	Q	Q	Q	R	R	R	S	S	S
5	S/T	T	T	T	U	U	U	V	V	V
6	V/W	W	W	W	X	X	X	X	Y	Y
7	Y	Y	Y	Y	Y/Z	Z	Z	Z	Z	Z
8	Z	Z	Z	Z	Z	Z	Z	Z	Z	Z
9–12	Z	Z	Z	Z+	Z+	Z+	Z+	Z+	Z+	Z+

Note. Based on Fountas and Pinnell (2010).

analysis also serves as one of the prescriptive keys for moving a child forward. What behaviors are dominating the child's error pattern? When he or she approaches the novel word, is the child forfeiting his or her knowledge of letter–sound relationships to substitute a theme-related word or is he or she forfeiting the sense of meaning and approximating a word with a few similar letters? Is he or she making the cognitive transfer that what he or she can do in writing can also be applied in reading? Is the child understanding that the purpose of phonics instruction is to be applied during reading connected text, or does he or she view tapping out sounds or adding macrons and breves in isolation as ends in themselves with little or no connection to reading? The whole point of phonics instruction is for it to kick in *invisibly* during connected text, meaningful reading. Young readers often do not create the bridge between phonics instruction and reading connected text. The use of decodable text is valuable in providing concentrated practice in particular patterns, but one can't assume that it will teach children to apply what they have learned during a series of phonics lessons to authentic text. Running records of text reading are necessary to document the novice reader's ability to read increasingly difficult text with fluency and comprehension.

For most students in kindergarten through early second grade, progress monitoring once a month can serve as the documentation of a child's growth trajectory. Monthly, formal documentation of literacy growth is adequate because we are assuming that at this stage of reading more informal text-level monitoring is happening by teachers in order to ensure that the child has readable texts in his or her hands. However, for the struggling reader, progress monitoring by the classroom teacher must occur more frequently: weekly or biweekly. As gatekeeper, the classroom teacher must bear this responsibility. The only exception is when the child is in a Reading Recovery setting where daily running records are occurring and high standards for movement are at the center of the instructional agenda. In this situation, the classroom teacher should be communicating weekly with the interventionist to ensure that the child is receiving the equivalent text-level instruction during differentiated instruction in the Tier 1 setting.

High-Frequency Words

Automatic recognition of the words that appear in texts with the highest frequency is an important foundational skill. Surprisingly, neither AIMSweb nor DIBELS Next provide CBMs for this skill. It is a skill that is easily taught and easily measured. Therefore, the classroom teachers in grades K–2 usually assume responsibility for monitoring acquisition of a collaboratively agreed-upon word list, typically subsets of the Dolch (1936) or Fry (1980) lists. Progress monitoring this skill can be easily accomplished during a small differentiated reading time slot or at some other odd time during the day (during independent reading, before school, writing workshop).

Because it is so easy to administer, minimal skill is required for the administration other than rigid adherence to standardized procedures (1-second allowance for automatic recognition).

During screening, children are assessed using the master list and instruction is driven from that list. For progress monitoring, monthly CBMs are administered using a commercially purchased set of lists or a free computer-generated list (*www.interventioncentral.org*). The important thing is not whether a school decides to use Fry (1980) or Dolch (1936), CBMs or a criterion-based list; the important thing is that these word lists are being taught to mastery for every child and that it is documented.

Additionally, because the results of this highly constrained skill are so easily interpreted and translated into instruction, this is a skill that does lend itself to employing the support of *trained* teaching assistants or uncertified personnel for assessment administration and practice drills. However, the classroom teacher is the gatekeeper and accountable for each child's mastery of the assigned list.

Oral Reading Fluency

Typically, in grades 2 through 5 children with fluency problems will be progress monitored as part of their Tier 2 experience. However, sometimes there are children in the intermediate grades who seem to be on track in all other areas of reading with the exception of reading rate. During differentiated instruction in the Tier 1 setting, these children are receiving fluency support. This might be taking the form of charted repeated reading, additional work with the automaticity of high-frequency words, or various forms of assisted reading. These practice activities provide opportunities for teachers to monitor reading rate informally. The classroom teacher will formally progress-monitor oral reading fluency of students with isolated reading-rate problems during the differentiated reading time slot using the grade-level progress monitoring CBMs provided by a commercial publisher on a monthly basis.

THE GATEKEEPER

In closing, the classroom educator's most important role in an RTI framework is that of gatekeeper. The Tier 1 teacher has an overview of all assessments and instruction for every child in his or her class. Only he or she knows the overall schedule. He or she needs to be competent and confident enough to set boundaries and advocate for his or her students. Both ongoing professional development and regular staff meetings between all teachers who work with the children can increase the likelihood of the Tier 1 teacher acting as child advocate when challenges arise. The teacher must feel confident enough to insist that a kindergarten EL child may not be pulled out of the classroom during the teacher read-aloud because of the language development and comprehension instruction that occur during that time frame. The teacher has to be competent and confident enough to recognize that the scripted phonics program that did not work for a child in Tier 2 is certainly inappropriate for that child as a Tier 3 or special education intervention. Each specialist is responsible for promoting a child's abilities in his or her area of specialization. However, the classroom teacher is responsible for nurturing the development of the whole child in a cohesive and comprehensive manner. Communication and ongoing professional development help to make this possible in increasingly refined ways.

Progress Monitoring Chart for Grades K–2

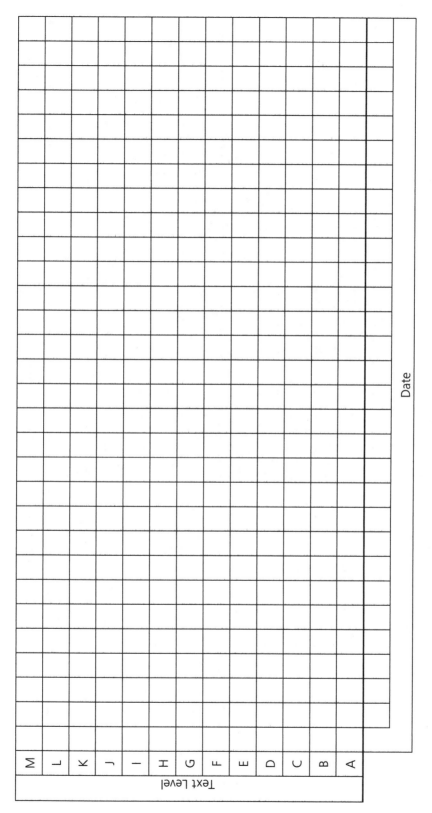

Date

Text Level

M
L
K
J
I
H
G
F
E
D
C
B
A

FORM 4.2

Progress Monitoring Chart for Grades 3–6

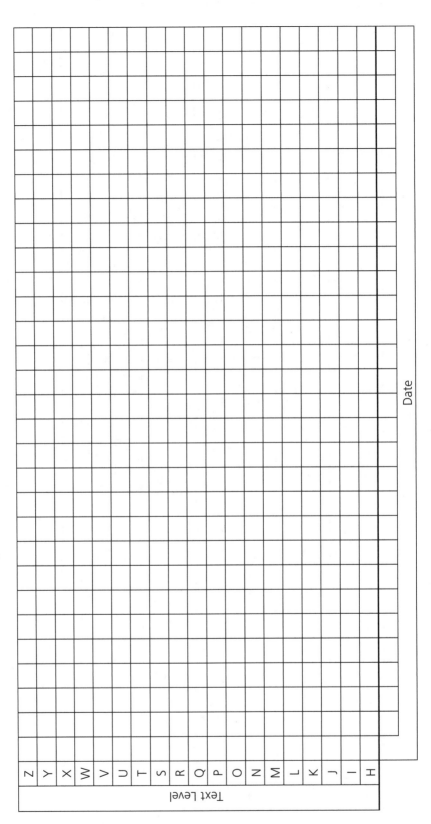

Date

CHAPTER FIVE

Assessments in Tier 2
Providing and Evaluating Secondary Support

Tier 2 is the supplementary small-group instruction provided to those children who are encountering reading difficulties despite exposure to research-based, comprehensive literacy instruction in the Tier 1 setting. Typically, 20% of a grade-level cohort might require this additional level of support. Most sources indicate that schools with more than 25–30% of their children not meeting instructional benchmarks need to evaluate the effectiveness of the existing Tier 1 comprehensive literacy instruction (Denton & Vaughn, 2010). Because the Tier 2 intervention is more intense and resource laden than Tier 1 instruction, it is designed to accommodate the needs of a relatively small percentage of students. It is unrealistic—and in fact logistically impossible—for a school to meet the needs of more than 30% of a grade-level cohort with the level of specialization and intensity required in Tier 2.

During Tier 2, the student receives additional instruction beyond that which is provided universally to all students. Let's assume, for example, that all of the children in a class receive 60 minutes of common literacy instruction plus 30 minutes of differentiated instruction in small groups. Tier 2 extends beyond the 90-minute comprehensive literacy block in an effort to provide data-driven, targeted instruction to a subset of struggling readers. It is based on the premise that struggling readers need *additional* support beyond the Tier 1 experience if they are ever to achieve grade-level benchmarks and catch up with their classmates who are performing at or above grade level. Because the instruction provided in Tier 1 (including differentiation) enables everyone to make progress, the gap between the children who are behind and those who are not cannot be bridged. If struggling children are to stand any chance of catching up, they need something extra.

In an ideal world, the moment a teacher recognizes that a child is encountering challenges in learning to read that are unmet by differentiation in the classroom setting, a problem-solving team with the support of a reading expert would devise a diagnostically driven, research-based intervention. The child would receive a small-group or individual intervention from a reflective, knowledgeable reading expert. This intervention might look like Reading Recovery (Clay, 2005) or the interactive strategies approach (Scanlon, Anderson, & Sweeney, 2010; Vellutino & Scanlon, 2002), two problem-solving interventions with strong research validation. Problem-solving approaches incorporate the use of individual diagnostics to determine a student's reading strengths and weaknesses. On this basis, teachers then develop an intervention to meet the student's needs. Frequent progress monitoring is applied to gauge the impact of the intervention and adjust it if necessary to ensure that the child is improving.

So much for an ideal world. The unfortunate truth is that application of problem-solving models requires a considerable amount of time and expertise. As a result, in troubled schools or schools that are beginning the RTI process with large numbers of children performing well below grade-level benchmarks, a problem-solving model can burden the diagnostic system beyond capacity. These schools simply do not have the resources, both financial and human, to carry off an effective diagnostically based intervention model for all of the Tier 2 students who need the second level of support. Even scheduling interventions with this level of student specificity will tax the system.

As a result, we address Tier 2 with the assumption that a standardized protocol is being employed. Those schools that are applying a problem-solving model in Tier 2 should follow the assessment recommendations provided for Tier 3 (see Chapter 6). For individually created interventions, the more rigid standards of progress monitoring associated with Tier 3 are appropriate to ensure that the student is growing.

We urge caution to school RTI planning teams who consider using classroom teachers to provide both effective Tier 1 instruction and Tier 2 intervention during the regular school day. Because of the heavy instructional burden on the Tier 1 teacher for providing a strong comprehensive literacy program, finding the time to provide a sustained, cohesive Tier 2 intervention (either problem-solving or standardized protocol) and monitor progress biweekly or weekly within the regular school day can be overwhelming and may compromise the effectiveness of both tiers. Often, classroom differentiation is forfeited. Still worse, on days when schedules are modified for special activities or early dismissal, the Tier 2 intervention is sacrificed altogether. An exception is when the school applies Title I funding to provide before- or after-school interventions that are well attended by the target recipients.

THE STANDARD-PROTOCOL APPROACH

A standardized protocol is a "specialized, scientifically based reading program(s)/ curricula" (Vaughn & Denton, 2008, p. 53) that is designed to meet particular students' needs. The standardized protocol often makes use of a specific program or set of commercial materials. Tier 2 instruction using a standardized protocol is usually provided to a heterogeneous group of three to six children 4–5 days a week for 20–40 minutes a day. It is always provided in addition to, not during or in place of, the 90- to 180-minute Tier 1 literacy block. It may be taught by the classroom teacher (though we have cautioned against it), a reading specialist, a special educator, or some other person trained to administer the standardized protocol. In some urban settings or in schools with financial restraints, the standardized protocol is taught in a very formalized, prescriptive (sometimes scripted) manner employing trained personnel whose only role in the school is to administer the program with fidelity and to conduct the program assessments and Tier 2 progress monitoring tasks.

Roberto Clemente Elementary School (pseudonym) is a high-poverty, low-achieving urban school. During the first 2 years of RTI implementation, the school had well over 50% of its first and second graders not meeting DIBELS Next screening benchmarks or district text-level benchmarks. Taking advantage of a commercial intervention program that was financially supported by the district and in alignment with the DIBELS assessments provided the fiscal freedom for this school to purchase a comprehensive core curriculum that would replace a "do-your-own-thing" classroom curriculum with a cohesive literacy program. Applying this Tier 2 model allowed the school to focus professional development efforts on improving both Tier 1 literacy instruction and fidelity to standardized assessment procedures. Additionally, it freed the reading specialists to work with the older Tier 3 students, who were among the school's neediest.

THE ROLE OF THE TIER 2 TEACHER

What is the difference between Tier 1 differentiation and Tier 2 instruction? The Tier 1 teacher is the gatekeeper responsible for the learning of *all* children in all subjects. Classroom differentiation ensures that everyone learns what is next on his or her personal developmental trajectory in each subject. *All* children are the recipients of instruction to meet particular learning needs. Accomplishing this feat isn't easy and requires that a teacher juggle a variety of needs and constraints. For example, the classroom teacher juggles the knowledge that Miguel needs to leave at 8:35 for his EL support, the fact that he also needs scaffolded instruction to support the process of moving from Text Level G to H, and his need for practice in applying his knowledge of short vowels in single-syllable words while reading connected text. His small-group differentiated instruction will address these needs. Additionally, it is imperative that Miguel is in classroom for the teacher read-aloud and shared reading so that he can receive the comprehension and conceptual vocabulary instruction that all children need, but with modifications to support learning English as a second language. José also leaves at 8:35 to go with the EL teacher, but his literacy skills are fairly sophisticated and he needs instruction in identifying the key elements of the narrative and informational Level L texts he is reading. His decoding challenges tend to occur with multisyllabic words and the less common vowel teams that he encounters when reading his new Level L texts. Tier 1 differentiation will ensure that each of these boys receives the rich instruction that will enable each to be challenged as a learner and to make at least a year of progress from different starting points. So even though differentiated instruction may focus on particular targeted skills, the Tier 1 teacher always has the whole child's development in view. This means that he or she is responsible for the child's comprehensive language and literacy development as well as growth in other disciplines and emotional well-being. This teacher is the child's advocate.

Tier 2 instruction is provided only to a subset of children who have not met particular achievement benchmarks. Children are placed in a Tier 2 setting based primarily on poor performance on a screening assessment. Therefore, the skills tested on that particular assessment should be the focus of Tier 2 instruction. Given the short amount of time that Tier 2 teachers have with students—20 to 40 minutes—instruction must be extremely focused on key teaching points if maximum benefits are to be realized. Moreover, the instructional pace must be brisk, activities well planned, and materials prepared and organized. Although some connected text reading is included in each session, the emphasis is on the application of targeted skills and strategies. The Tier 2 teacher actually relies on the Tier 1 teacher to help the child integrate newly learned isolated skills into the more holistic literacy acts of reading and writing connected texts of varying genres for multiple purposes. Collaboration between the two teachers is essential. The time allocation for Tier 2 instruction is long enough to teach foundational skills intensely and thoroughly, but it does not include enough time to adapt them to a wide range of authentic contexts. That needs to occur in Tier 1 and it is one of the reasons that Tier 1 differentiated instruction must be a priority. It often serves as the bridge between Tier 2 and Tier 1 whole-class literacy instruction.

Based on the screening data and other information collected by the Tier 1 teacher, a child might be assigned to a Tier 2 intervention. Typically, the intervention would focus on phonemic awareness and phonics, phonics and fluency, fluency and comprehension, or comprehension. It is more intense than Tier 1 differentiation in size of group (three to six students), frequency and duration, and focus on specific targeted skills with fidelity checks to ensure strict adherence to the standardized protocol. To aid them in the selection of a standardized protocol for each of those constructs, many schools use the What Works Clearinghouse, the Best Evidence Encyclopedia, or other websites that review the effectiveness of commercial programs and procedures. For example, schools with a core program might use the intervention materials that come with their core package. Schools without a core program often use something like Fundations for the children with phonemic awareness and phonics problems in K–3, Wilson Phonics in grades 4 and 5 for children with phonics and fluency problems in the upper grades, RAVE-O (Retrieval, Automaticity, Vocabulary, Engagement–Orthography; Morris et al., 2012; Wolf, Miller, & Donnelly, 2000; Wolf & Segal, 1999) for comprehension and fluency problems, and Collaborative Strategic Reading (Klingner, Vaughn, Arguelles, Hughes, & Leftwich, 2004; Klingner, Vaughn, Hughes, Schumm, & Elbaum, 1998; Klingner, Vaughn, & Schumm, 1998) for comprehension. The effectiveness of Tier 2 is reliant on the formation of small homogeneous groups of children with common needs receiving an intervention that addresses those needs.

Keeping a tight focus on particular skills in Tier 2 allows those children who were confused in the classroom or simply a bit behind to catch on and catch up. Both the explicitness of the instruction and the focus on particular skills enable children who have the capacity to learn the skill to achieve mastery. Given such direct instruction and intense practice, the small percentage of children who still aren't making acceptable levels of practice become the candidates for the diagnostic, individualized instruction that will become available in Tier 3. Tier 3 applies the diagnostic, problem-solving protocol. As a result, it is resource expensive and must be reserved for a few children with the most severe reading problems.

TIER 2 ASSESSMENT

Screening

The Tier 2 teachers need to be experts in CBM testing. Their knowledge enables them to lend great support to the Tier 1 teachers during CBM screening. They can participate in the screening process as members of the testing SWAT team or paired with particular teachers to accelerate the testing process. Having the Tier 1 and Tier 2 teachers work together to administer the CBM screening tasks accomplishes multiple goals.

- *It speeds up the testing process.* Having two persons testing is sensible because it cuts the testing time in half. And in our experience pairing the testers can actually cut the testing time by *more* than 50%. When two teachers work together, they are more vigilant in adhering to a rigorous test schedule because they are working around another person's schedule. When a teacher is working on his or her own schedule, any number of interruptions or distractions can get in the way of sticking to a testing agenda. These tests need to be administered within a narrow time frame and to interrupt teaching as little as possible. See Figure 5.1 for a sample testing and instructional schedule.

• *It fosters collaboration and communication between tiers.* The more opportunities that Tier 1 and Tier 2 teachers have to work together and talk together about children and data, the greater the likelihood that children will receive the help they need. It provides an opportunity for the Tier 2 teacher to be in the Tier 1 classroom setting to communicate with the classroom teacher informally about the students in all risk categories. Having an overview of the screening data for all children expands the Tier 2 teacher's perspective. It helps the teacher see which children might fit together well within homogeneous Tier 2 groups. It provides a lens for viewing children who are on the brink between Tier 1 and Tier 2. It also opens the door for communication between the two teachers about the cohesiveness of content in the Tier 1 and Tier 2 setting even before any formal data meetings occur.

• *It increases the likelihood of fidelity to standardized testing procedures.* When schools implement an RTI framework and apply the recommended practices regarding training for standardized test administration, the reliability of test results does increase. However, partnering teachers also increases the likelihood that standardized procedures will be applied consistently. Hearing and seeing someone else follow the script is affirmation of the expectation. Knowing that test data will be reviewed closely by a partner decreases the sense of freedom to alter or take shortcuts with testing procedures. Additionally, it fosters an atmosphere of convenience and safety that allows teachers to ask each other questions about test administration and scoring procedures. When errors are made, they are quickly identified and corrected. So although the Tier 2 teachers should not be considered the CBM police, their experience using CBMs on a weekly basis can provide classroom teachers with a convenient support system during administration of the periodic screening tests.

Fall screening 2 weeks		Fall semester		Winter screening 1 week	Winter semester		Spring screening 1 week
	Tier 1 Differentiation	16 weeks 5 rounds × 3 weeks			16 weeks 5 rounds × 3 weeks		
	Tier 2	F1 8 weeks	F2 8 weeks		W1 8 weeks	W2 8 weeks	
	Tier 3	F1 8 weeks	F2 8 weeks		W1 8 weeks	W2 8 weeks	

FIGURE 5.1. An RTI calendar.

Diagnostic Assessments

Because of the specialized role of the Tier 2 teacher when applying a standard protocol intervention, the only informal or diagnostic measures that he or she may need to give would be those that are part of the standardized program. For example, many of the intervention components of core programs or commercial intervention programs include brief diagnostic measures to determine the right level of instruction and weekly or unit criterion measures to assess mastery of specific skills. The Tier 2 teacher would be responsible for using these assessments selected by the RTI design team during the audit process and monitoring Tier 2 instruction according to program directives.

Progress Monitoring

Managing Progress Monitoring

The Tier 2 teachers' most demanding assessment task is the administration, scoring, and interpretation of the tests used for progress monitoring. Typically, schools progress-monitor biweekly in Tier 2. However, although "there are no hard and fast rules for the frequency of progress monitoring, it should be increased when the content is important and the student is at risk for academic problems" (Hosp et al., 2007, p. 124). If the Tier 2 teacher is concerned about certain children's progress on particularly important skills, he or she may see a need to adjust the frequency from biweekly to weekly. In grades K–3, most of these tasks are individually administered. Data management systems help to make record keeping and graphing the results easier, but in many high-poverty schools these tasks must be managed using pen and paper.

Maintaining a Focus

Progress monitoring tasks replicate those that are administered during the screening process (see Table 5.1). In the earlier grades, individual administration of the foundational skills tests results in most schools teaching for 4 days or 9 days (i.e., 1 week or 2 prior to testing) and then devoting 1 day to progress monitoring. This practice is fairly routine because the instruction most children receive is similar. However, as children grow older and their needs become more diverse, monitoring their progress becomes trickier.

In grades 3–5, it is likely that the focus of intervention groups will vary widely. In addition to needing separate groups to address the needs of children who are still requiring a heavy emphasis on phonics/fluency as opposed to those who primarily need support in comprehension, there may be different developmental levels of need within those groups. This means that in the upper grades different children will need different measures of ongoing progress. For example, in third

TABLE 5.1. Assessments to Inform Tier 2 Instruction

Type of assessment	Task	Administration	Frequency
Screening (conducted in tandem with classroom teacher)	CBM prescribed by grade level and school	Individual	3 × per year
Diagnostics	Program-prescribed	Program-prescribed	Program-prescribed
Progress monitoring	CBMs specific to targeted skills	Individual	Biweekly or weekly
	High-frequency words (as needed in grades 3–4)	Individual	Weekly

and possibly fourth grade some of the children who are scoring poorly on the measure of oral reading fluency may still need work on acquiring automaticity of the high-frequency words. At this point, most children in the regular classroom will have mastered these words. Therefore, the Tier 2 teacher will need both to teach and progress-monitor this skill. However, not every child in the Tier 2 setting will continue to require this particular focus. Situations like this illustrate the fact that although Tier 2 may be standardized, teachers will still need to accommodate the differences among children, differences that are sure to become more pronounced each year.

As seen in Table 5.2, progress monitoring needs to be specific to children's needs. There needs to a close match between poor screening outcomes and the instructional intervention. If, for example, particular children have achieved proficiency levels in letter recognition, the intervention should not involve spending time having all children call out the names of letters in a routinized manner, nor should those children continue to be progress monitored on letter names. Similarly, if a child is in an intervention because of comprehension difficulties, he or she should not be placed in a phonics program, and progress monitoring should include retelling or related tasks. Though this may sound like common sense, our experience is that some schools invest in a commercial phonics program and everybody with a reading problem receives heavy doses of phonics whether they need it or not.

The intervention minutes are too valuable to be wasted on what the child already knows or on skills that are beyond the child's zone of proximal development (ZPD), which consists of tasks that a child can't do alone, but can do with assistance. Tier 2 settings should provide intense instruction occurring at the high end of each child's ZPD. For this reason, groups should range in size from three to six students. Groups of this size increase the likelihood of homogeneity with regard to the targeted instruction. It is also hard to imagine that a Tier 2 teacher could complete the required progress monitoring for more than six children per group.

TABLE 5.2. Progress Monitoring Tasks

Grade	Screening	Intervention focus	Progress monitoring	Time of administration
K	Letter names	Letter recognition	Letter names	F1, F2, W1, W2
	Phoneme segmentation	Phonemic awareness	Phoneme segmentation	W1, W2
	Nonsense words	Letter–sound relationships (phonics)	Nonsense words	W1, W2
1	Letter names	Letter recognition	Letter names	As needed
	Phoneme segmentation	Phonemic awareness	Phoneme segmentation	F1, F2, W1, W2
	Nonsense words	Phonics	Nonsense words	F1, F2, W1, W2
	Oral reading fluency (ORF)	Fluency	ORF	W, as needed
2	Phoneme segmentation	Phonemic awareness	Phoneme segmentation	F1, F2
	Nonsense words	Phonics	Nonsense words	F1, F2, W1, W2
	ORF	Fluency	ORF	F1, F2, W1, W2
3	ORF	High-frequency words (HFW)	HFW	As needed
	ORF	Phonics		
	ORF	Fluency	ORF	F1, F2, W1, W2
	Maze/daze	Comprehension	Maze/daze	As needed
4	ORF	HFW	HFW	As needed
	Maze/daze	Phonics		
		Fluency	ORF	F1, F2, W1, W2
		Comprehension	Maze/daze	As needed
5	ORF	Phonics	ORF	As needed
	Maze/daze	Fluency	ORF	As needed
		Comprehension	Maze/daze	

Establishing a Goal

The use of graphs, whether computer generated or created manually, makes the progress monitoring data easy to interpret. The vertical axis typically reflects the particular content of the graph, and the horizontal axis reflects the cycle or dates of administration. In other words, the vertical axis always represents skill level and the horizontal axis always denotes time. Figure 5.2 shows a simple graph for words read correctly per minute (WRC[1]) for Rufous, a second grader. This graph provides

---

[1] This abbreviation is used by DIBELS Next. It is the same as WCPM.

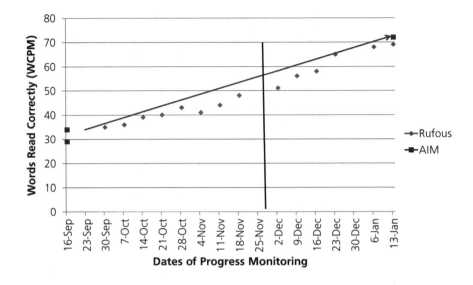

FIGURE 5.2. Oral reading fluency progress monitoring.

a quick view of both performance level and progress rate. The most common way to set a performance goal is to use the mid- or end-of-year benchmark (see Table 5.3) or the 50th percentile rank (Hosp et al., 2007). The goal for Rufous was established using the midyear second-grade Hasbrouck and Tindal (2006) norms (see Table 5.4). Once the instructional goal has been established, a line is drawn from the baseline data point to the goal. This is considered the aim line. Each student's progress monitoring data are recorded on his or her individual graph in comparison to his or her aim line. For consistency and ease of interpretation, the same graph needs to be used for each student. The increments for content need to be small enough to reflect sensitive levels of growth, but not so small that they magnify small units of growth. Naturally, each increment must be identical.

TABLE 5.3. Benchmarks for DIBELS Next ORF CBM (2010)

Grade	Beginning of year WRC/accuracy %/retell	Midyear WRC/accuracy %/retell	End of year WRC/accuracy %/retell
1	NA/NA/NA	23/78/NA	47/90/15
2	52/90/16	72/96/21	87/97/27
3	70/95/20	86/96/26	100/97/30
4	90/96/27	103/97/30	115/98/33
5	111/98/33	120/98/36	130/99/36
6	107/97/27	109/97/29	120/98/32

TABLE 5.4. Fiftieth Percentile Ranks for ORF CBM in Words Read Correctly

Grade	AIMSweb (2006)			Hasbrouck and Tindal (2006)		
	Fall	Winter	Spring	Fall	Winter	Spring
1	8	23	52	n/a	23	53
2	54	77	92	51	72	89
3	77	96	110	71	92	107
4	99	114	126	94	112	123
5	112	128	141	110	127	139
6	131	144	155	127	140	150
7	131	140	153	128	136	150
8	138	146	155	133	146	151

Note. This measure is the same as WCPM.

To create an individual student's graph for a particular target, plot the student's baseline data on the far left of the graph. In school settings, the child's screening data are used as the baseline. In special education, Tier 3, or a reading clinic, the individual scores for three assessments may be administered and charted on the same horizontal axis using the middle point as the baseline. Using the median of three scores provides a slightly more accurate baseline.

> As an example, let's consider Paul, who enters second grade with an AIMSweb ORF score of 44 WRC. This score is well below the fall AIMSweb 50th percentile rank of 54 WRC. Following the cognitive model, Paul's Tier 2 teacher first conducts additional assessments of decoding and high-frequency words to rule out these areas as the cause of his fluency problem. Let's assume that the teacher discovers no substantive difficulties in these areas and therefore makes a plan to target fluency directly. To gauge the effectiveness of the intervention, the teacher plots a straight-line trajectory representing the normal developmental path for second graders from the beginning of second grade to midyear, where the 50th percentile rank is 77 WRC. Figure 5.3 shows how the teacher has added this aim line to the blank graph in Figure 5.2, along with Paul's fall screening score. As an initial goal, the Tier 2 teacher may strive to get Paul's performance close to the aim line after an 8-week intervention. If more time is needed, values can be added to the chart each week. Of course, the data points along the way will help the Tier 2 teacher judge Paul's responsiveness to the intervention and possibly signal a need to try a different approach.

Some districts have enough long-term data that they have established their own local norms. Districts that have engaged in this process may encourage the use of local norms for goal setting. However, if local norms are lower than national

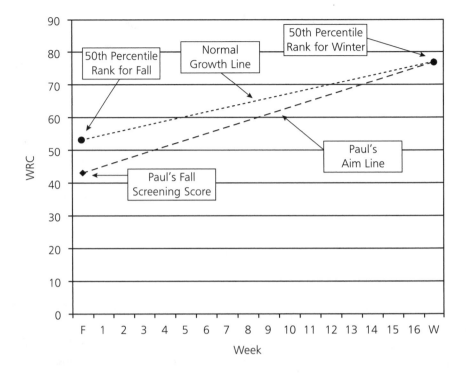

FIGURE 5.3. Paul's progress monitoring chart aim line for oral reading fluency.

norms, caution is urged in making judgments about student proficiency based on those standards. For this reason, the use of national norms is recommended.

Alternatively, a goal can be established using average weekly gain (Deno, Fuchs, Marston, & Shin, 2001; Fuchs, Fuchs, Hamlett, Walz, & Germann, 1993). This approach is more commonly used for ORF and maze than for other reading tasks due to the availability of typical growth rate norms. Table 5.5 discriminates between *realistic* goals and *ambitious* goals for ORF. The realistic goals are based on the growth rates for large groups of students, both with and without disabilities. The ambitious goal is based on a calculation that adds one standard deviation to the typical growth rate. If a student is receiving targeted instruction in an individualized setting, one might expect ambitious outcomes in an effort to narrow the performance gap. Fuchs and colleagues (1993) determined that the slope of growth for ORF decreased over time, whereas the slope of growth for comprehension, as reflected by maze, was consistent across time. Fuchs and Fuchs (2004) established 0.4 words correctly restored as an ambitious growth rate target for maze tasks in all grades. Although constrained skills theory had not been defined at the time of this study, Fuchs and colleagues apply a similar developmental theory to explain their findings. Due to the complexity of comprehension and the fact that students encounter texts of increasing complexity throughout their schooling, growth rates

TABLE 5.5. Weekly Growth Rates for ORF CBM: Words Read Correctly

Grade	Realistic weekly growth rates (WRC)[a]	Ambitious weekly growth rates (WRC)[a]
1	2	3
2	1.5	2
3	1	1.5
4	0.85	1.1
5	.5	0.8
6	.3	0.65

[a]Data from Fuchs et al. (1993).

tend to be consistent across the years. However, ORF is more strongly influenced by growth in word-recognition abilities that increase most rapidly in the early grades and reach a ceiling as children get older, thus the decreasing growth rates throughout the intermediate grades. Evidence of how fluency plateaus in the upper grades is evident from Table 5.4. The end-of-year 50th percentile rank for Hasbrouck and Tindal (2006) is 150 WRC in sixth grade, 150 in seventh, and 151 in eighth. Such a result makes sense because students do not simply read faster and faster until they reach auctioneer speed. Instead, their rate levels off when they arrive at a normal conversational rate. This gradual leveling-off makes fluency a moderately constrained skill.

MOVING: FORWARD, BACKWARD, OR STANDING STILL?

The application of a rigorous, standardized protocol focusing on a few target skills with extreme consistency and intensity provides a window for viewing whether or not the child successfully learns those skills. Such an approach makes the establishment of decision rules and the ramifications of those decision rules more clear-cut.

In looking at student data, we are interested in student performance and progress. In analyzing performance, we are looking at a child's level of *performance* compared to his or her grade level or age peers using a benchmark, percentile rank, or some other norm. However, we also want to consider a child's *rate of progress*. In order to analyze rate of progress, we need data sets obtained from frequent progress monitoring. Generally, progress can be gauged based on an examination of six to eight data points. Within this set of data points, four consecutive scores that fall above or below the aim line call for an adjustment (Fuchs, Fuchs, & Hamlett, 2007; Hosp et al., 2007). AIMSweb recommends using three consecutive scores within a set of six data points as a progress indicator.

If the points consistently fall below the aim line, it indicates that some instructional modification is required. Lowering the goal is not an option (Hosp et al., 2007). Changes in the intervention need to be indicated on the graph using a vertical line (see Figure 5.2). Given 8 weeks of intervention and weekly progress monitoring, more than four consecutive points were below the aim line. This indicated that an intervention modification was in order for Rufous. Intensifying the intervention can be accomplished by altering the duration, frequency, group size, or the instructional techniques. The vertical line indicates the date of the intervention change. In Rufous's case, the change in intervention resulted in an ascending shift in progress toward the aim line.

If the scores are consistently above the aim line, the goal can be raised. Because of the urgency for children who are performing below grade level, it is important to ascertain if the remediation efforts are working before an excessive amount of time has passed. Adjustments to the intensity of the intervention are made by modifying frequency, duration, group size, amount and kind of corrective feedback, specificity of goals, and instructor's expertise (Mellard, McKnight, & Jordan, 2010). These adjustments may be made within tiers or moving across tiers. This reasoning is at the heart of RTI.

As part of the assessment audit and development process, the RTI design team should formulate a decision tree that includes when the decision points will occur and the number of consecutive scores above or below the aim line that will be used as the guideline for initiating an intervention adjustment. Some sample plans that are currently being used by schools throughout the state of New York may be found on the state RTI Technical Assistance website (*www.nysrti.org/page/pilot-schools*). Figure 5.4 displays one New York school's decision tree. An exploration of the plans being utilized by 14 very different schools demonstrates how each school's ecological characteristics influence this process.

Rounds of Instruction

There are many opinions about the number of 8-week intervention rounds that children should undergo before transitioning back to the classroom or into Tier 3 for more individualized, intensive assistance. Some recommend just two rounds of intervention, with instructional modifications, before shifting to Tier 3 or even referral for evaluation for special education (Brown-Chidsey & Steege, 2005). Others have provided multiple rounds of tiered interventions with modifications for increasing intensity before referring for special education (Vellutino, Scanlon, & Lyon, 2000; Vellutino et al., 1996). Our perusal of articles, state guidance recommendations, and books confirms the wide range of opinions on this issue. As a result, this is one of the areas that is most confusing to schools. Unfortunately, the confusion can keep the children who need help most urgently sitting in unproductive layers of tiered instruction for years. Alternatively, it can keep children who are outside

Woodside's Decision Rules

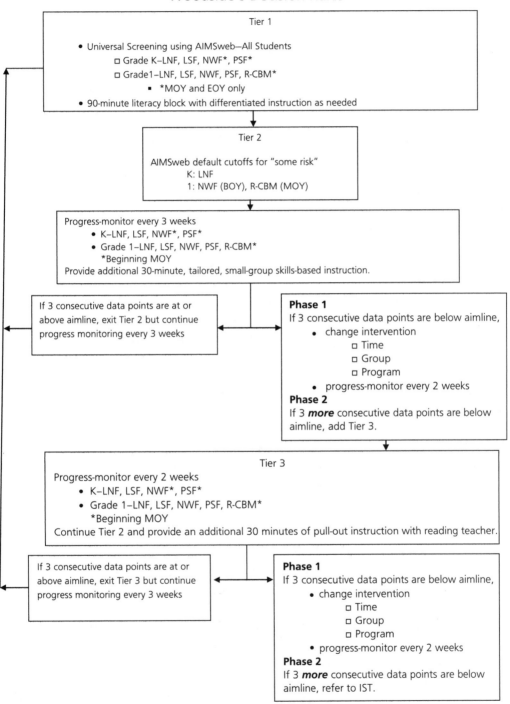

FIGURE 5.4. Sample decision tree from a New York school.

risk categories sitting in intervention settings unnecessarily, in the process missing classroom instruction and enlarging intervention groups (K. A. D. Stahl & Keane, 2010). One rationale for buying into the RTI paradigm is to eliminate the "wait to fail" and "learning to be disabled" mentality that became associated with the IQ-achievement discrepancy model of special education identification. The goal of RTI is to keep children who do not need special education outside the system, especially children of linguistic and racial diversity who are often disproportionately categorized as in need of special education services. However, RTI was never intended to prevent children from receiving the benefits of special services when called for.

Research has not yet defined and is unlikely to define any hard-and-fast rules about numbers of rounds of tiered intervention, because these decisions largely rely on the ecological variations within a school or district. These decisions depend on the format and resources available within each unique RTI framework. However, to avoid children sitting in preliminary tiers for years when they really need the individualized, specialized, and sustained services provided by special education funding, clean decision point policies must be defined by the school RTI team with room for negotiation.

For example, a school that has a full-service Reading Recovery program in first grade with trained Reading Recovery teachers providing a problem-solving model of Tier 2 support in kindergarten and second grade, can be fairly confident in referring a child for formal evaluation for special education if the child demonstrates a dual discrepancy (low performance and low rates of progress) after two or three rounds of intense, research-validated intervention by the reading expert. In fact, such a school would need to work hard to provide special education services that are equally or more intense and individualized than the tiered intervention. On the other hand, a school that is applying a standardized Tier 2 program followed by the problem-solving Tier 3 intervention may need to supply a total of three or four rounds of secondary and tertiary interventions before being able to conclude that that child's dual discrepancy is likely to require the sustained, individualized, and specialized support and accommodations provided through special education. A red flag needs to be raised and pointed conversations need to address the needs of children who have been in Tier 2 or Tier 3 interventions for longer than three rounds. Schools need to decide how to allocate resources to provide for the needs of the children who have the most difficulty. Suggesting that parents recruit outside help is not the answer.

In reviewing data, a school must be cautious that they avoid the premature celebration of lower special education referral rates and placements. Many schools that have implemented an RTI model have reduced their special education referral rates not only because fewer children needed special education services but because teachers were no longer permitted to make special education referrals; instead, children needed to go through the tiered process, and the authority to make referral decisions was vested with a group defined within the RTI framework (K. A. D. Stahl, 2009; K. A. D. Stahl & Keane, 2010). In these schools, this policy resulted in reductions in special education placements, to be sure, but also in referral delays for those children who clearly needed the accommodations provided within special education. Unfortunately for some children, it also resulted in retentions because children did not pass the statewide tests necessary for promotion to the next grade level or because primary teachers saw retention as the best way to meet the needs of children who continued to perform well below grade level.

CHAPTER SIX

Assessments in Tier 3 and Beyond
Diagnostic Decision Making

Tier 3 is reserved for the children with reading difficulties that are difficult to remediate. These students require the support provided by a teacher with expertise in reading development, research-based instructional techniques, and reading assessment. In Table 6.1 we present a list of assessments and the functions they serve in Tier 3. Most of these tend to be time consuming and schools typically have only a few teachers with this level of expertise. Therefore, Tier 3 intervention must be reserved for a small number of children. The suggestions in this chapter are applicable to schools that do have several reading experts and apply a diagnostic problem-solving model to develop each struggling reader's Tier 2 intervention. The suggestions are also appropriate for developing an individualized education plan (IEP) in special education.

THE PROBLEM-SOLVING APPROACH

Children may arrive in Tier 3 by one of two routes. Some children arrive after Tier 2 interventions have proved unsuccessful in producing adequate rates of progress and achievement levels. Other children arrive in Tier 3 as the result of alarmingly low screening outcomes. For example, children who are categorized in the high-risk categories of DIBELS Next or below the 11th percentile rank on AIMSweb assessment task might skip a standardized Tier 2 intervention and be placed immediately in the diagnostically driven Tier 3 intervention. Figure 6.1 illustrates these paths.

Because the needs of these children are so severe, the Tier 3 intervention is typically provided 5 days a week for 45–60 minutes beyond the Tier 1 comprehensive

TABLE 6.1. Assessments to Inform Tier 3 Instruction

Type of assessment	Task	Administration	Frequency
Screening[a]	TOWRE: Phonemic Decoding and Sight Word Efficiency	Individual	3× per year
	IRI Full Administration: all levels with mixed genres (determine independent, instructional, frustration and listening capacity levels; analysis of retelling and question-answering ability)	Individual	Full, upon entry Instructional level, 3× per year
Diagnostics (selected tasks based on screening indicators)	Tests of Phonemic Awareness (McKenna & Stahl, 2009)	Individual	As needed
	Writing Vocabulary (Clay, 2006)		
	Informal Phonics Inventory (McKenna & Stahl, 2009)		
	Z-Test (McKenna & Stahl, 2009)		
	Wordless Picture Book (McKenna & Stahl, 2009)		
	Strategic Reading Interview (McKenna & Stahl, 2009)		
	Reading Attitude Survey and Activity Interviews (McKenna & Stahl, 2009)		
Progress monitoring	CBMs specific to targeted skills (with grade-level adjustments, as needed)	Individual	Weekly
	Text reading level (K–2)	Individual	Weekly
	High-frequency word inventories (as needed in grades 3–4)	Individual	Weekly
	Retelling idea units (as needed in grades 3–6)	Individual	As needed
Normed standardized (optional)	Woodcock–Johnson Achievement Battery	Individual	One time
	Peabody Picture Vocabulary Test–IV		
	Expressive Vocabulary Test–2		

[a]These assessments are not used in the same way we employ screening assessments at Tiers 1 and 2. Those listed above are more focused and fine grained but are still likely to require diagnostic follow-up. For this reason they serve a screening function.

literacy block. The group size ranges from one to three students with highly homogeneous diagnostic profiles. Progress monitoring occurs weekly or even more frequently. These logistical demands also dictate that this service be provided to a relatively small percentage of students within a grade-level cadre or school. Reading interventions such as Reading Recovery and the Interactive Strategies Approach (Scanlon et al., 2010) might be applied for children in the primary grades. A diagnostic or problem-solving model in Tier 3 serves two key functions. First, it provides students with the most intense level of intervention during a limited time frame by a

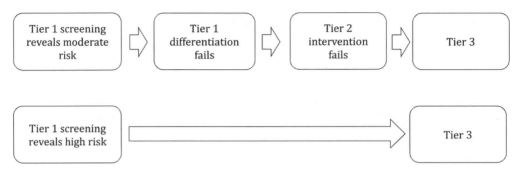

FIGURE 6.1. Decision paths leading to Tier 3.

reading teacher with the highest level of expertise. Second, it may serve as a bridge to a special education referral for students requiring long-term individualized support. These two functions drive the assessment process within Tier 3.

Using Diagnosis to Hit an Instructional Bull's-Eye

Tier 3 mirrors the diagnostic individualization and intensity originally intended for special education services. Diagnostic assessments provide detailed information to the teacher regarding what the student can and cannot do in particular skill areas. Without determining where the process is breaking down, a teacher can only apply a general intervention approach and hope that something works. The more finely grained assessments within each reading construct allow teachers to provide more finely grained instruction, increasing the likelihood of hitting the instructional target and, as a result, promoting accelerated progress. Using Table 6.1, a teacher can select the diagnostic tools that will provide detailed information about the reading difficulty that is indicated by the screening task. In-depth diagnosis is used to inform refined instructional modifications including adjustments to the content, pace, and delivery of instruction. For example, a first-grade child scoring in the highest risk category on DIBELS Next PSF and NWF might be selected to receive Tier 3 services. The Tier 3 teacher would then perform specific diagnostic assessments such as the Tests of Phonemic Awareness and Informal Phonics Inventory (McKenna & Stahl, 2009), as well as Writing Vocabulary (Clay, 2006) to provide the specific details needed to inform the content of Tier 3 instruction. The Tier 3 teacher uses diagnostic data in conjunction with the early literacy data collected by the classroom teacher to create an individualized instructional program for the child.

While this individualized protocol might include one or more components of a commercial program for the development of a particular skill, it is unlikely at this level of crisis that a single kit can be used as the entire instructional intervention. Because instruction is provided individually (or to a homogeneous group of three or fewer children), skills that the child needs to be taught are delivered using deliberately selected instructional techniques at a pace that is tailored to the child's needs. At this tier, we fit the instruction to the child, rather than requiring that the child fit into a program or curriculum. Moreover, the assessments that typically accompany a commercial program may be too few to gauge the near-term impact of Tier 3 instruction. Because each student's intervention protocol is individualized due to an instructional crisis, frequent progress monitoring is the only way to ensure that the instruction is working.

Commercial products warrant another caution as well: the possibility of overuse. Research-based instructional techniques are applied during the intervention sessions. Schools need to ensure that commercial programs that have been attempted unsuccessfully during earlier tiers are not reused in Tier 3 or special education.

At this tier, we cannot emphasize too strongly that the teacher must be a reading expert. Research syntheses have determined that effective reading interventions do not need to "come in a box" but do share a few common characteristics (Connor, Morrison, & Katch, 2004; Taylor, Pearson, Clark, & Walpole, 2000; Taylor, Peterson, Pearson, & Rodriguez, 2002; Vaughn, Gersten, & Chard, 2000; Wanzek & Vaughn, 2010):

- Instruction is explicit and systematic.
- Direct instruction is balanced with coaching and a range of support that allows for a gradual release of responsibility to the students.
- Procedures for self-regulation facilitate learning.
- Instruction incorporates an interactive orientation that honors both the foundational skills of reading and the comprehension of text.
- Challenging, motivating activities promote student engagement.
- Students have opportunities to apply isolated skills and strategies with a range of texts through reading, writing, and discussion.
- Intervention yields its largest effects when instruction is applied in a 1:1 setting as opposed to a small-group setting.
- Intervention yields its largest effects when conducted in kindergarten and first grade.

Additionally, Tier 3 requires a greater incorporation of reading and writing connected text than is necessary in Tier 2. Typically, children in Tier 3 are reading many levels below the grade-level expectation so they are probably doing less reading in the classroom and at home than their peers. The extended time committed to Tier 3 allows for specific isolated skill instruction, but it should also provide the time for children to receive instructional coaching in the application of those skills while reading a range of texts (Common Core State Standards Initiative, 2010). Many children functioning at this level do not remember or understand how to apply the component skills and strategies during an authentic reading experience. Therefore, the Tier 3 teacher must incorporate a range of connected reading experiences that are developmentally appropriate within the Tier 3 setting to maximize the likelihood of success (Wanzek & Vaughn, 2010).

Without intervention and deliberate, targeted attention, the gap in the volume of reading between struggling and successful readers increases over time (Juel, 1988; Stanovich, 1986). Tier 3 must intentionally diminish that gap rather than perpetuate it by focusing only on isolated skills or providing reading material that is too easy relative to the high degree of scaffolding provided in the 1:1, 1:2, or 1:3 setting. Remember that raising the amount of instructional scaffolding raises the student's instructional reading level (S. A. Stahl & Heubach, 2005). After all, the instructional level is so named because a student can comprehend so long as adequate instruction is provided. As Figure 6.2 makes clear, this level is not fixed but is always relative to instruction. For this reason, Nicholas Silvaroli, one of the pioneers of the IRI, preferred the term *instructional range* (Silvaroli, 1976). At the high end of this range, of course, frustration can be expected regardless of the instruction provided. Short of this point, however, Tier 3 students can begin to experience what it is like to comprehend challenging text as long as they have a capable instructor to lean on. This way of thinking is consistent with the Common Core Standards (2010) advocacy for the inclusion of texts that span wide *complexity bands.*

With this intensity of instructional scaffolding, the child can be pushed to perform in the higher end of the instructional range (or ZPD), actually verging on the frustrational reading level that may have been identified through assessment. For example, a third grader who has an independent reading level of I (Fountas & Pinnell, 2006, 2010), an instructional level of J (96% accuracy), and who has exhibited

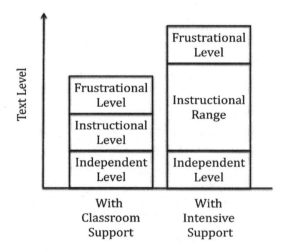

FIGURE 6.2. Instructional range.

frustration (88% accuracy) when tested using a Level K text, might be nudged into Level K texts during Tier 3 instruction because of the high degree of instructional support provided in a 1:1 setting compared to a classroom instructional setting. Reading with Level I and J texts would also be included with the expectation that less scaffolding would be provided by the teacher.

Instruction that addresses conceptual vocabulary, builds oral language, and provides opportunities for children to express their comprehension by retelling stories and summarizing informational texts is good for all children but essential for the EL. In order to break the pattern of disproportional grade-level retentions and special education referrals of ELs, the effective Tier 3 intervention creates the conditions for children to talk about text (Linan-Thompson, Cirino, & Vaughn, 2007; Linan-Thompson, Vaughn, Prater, & Cirino, 2006; Orosco & Klingner, 2010).

Table 6.2 lists some of the types of connected-text reading that fit within the intervention time frame and target the developmental needs of students at each grade level. Each form of reading might be applied for 15–20 minutes of the intervention period. Research indicates that these methods tend to increase the achievement in the areas that diagnostic assessment has led the teacher to target in each grade level. Each type of reading is aligned with the instructional goal and aligned with the assessment process for that developmental stage.

TABLE 6.2. Developmentally Appropriate Types of Reading for Tier 3

Student reading level	Activity	Function	Research support
K–2	Reading a range of increasingly difficult little books at the instructional level	Help children orchestrate comprehension and word-identification processes into a cohesive, fluent reading process	Clay (2005); Pinnell, Lyons, Deford, Bryk, & Seltzer (1994)
1–2	Decodable texts	Provide practice recognition and automaticity of orthographic patterns	Mesmer (2001); Walpole & McKenna (2007, 2009)
2–3	Assisted reading (echo reading, choral reading) of authentic grade-level texts (e.g., trade books, hypertext, poetry—but *not* decodable or predictable text)	Fluency, vocabulary, comprehension	Kuhn et al. (2010); S. A. Stahl & Heubach (2005)
3–6	Charted reading of short passages (100–300 words)	Fluency	Dowhower (1987); Samuels (1979)
4–6	Paired reading of authentic texts	Fluency, vocabulary, comprehension	Topping & Bryce (2004); Topping, Miller, Thurston, McGavok, & Conlin (2011)

Tier 3 as a Bridge to Special Education

In many cases, Tier 3 will serve as the bridge to special education. This becomes increasingly true over time as a school improves its core instruction, classroom differentiation, and tiered interventions during the RTI implementation process. The nature of children who arrive in Tier 3 will shift from those who simply were never explicitly taught how to read to those who have actual reading disabilities (Fuchs, Stecker, & Fuchs, 2008; Pedron, 1996; Wanzek & Vaughn, 2011). The true percentage of children appropriately referred for special education after Tier 3 is somewhat unclear. While some research studies have found that only 2–6% of the general population need special education after tiers of intense intervention (McMaster, Fuchs, Fuchs, & Compton, 2002; Torgesen, 2000; Vellutino et al., 2000), Fuchs and colleagues (2008) assume that figure is too low when RTI is implemented by practitioners as opposed to researchers with an isolated agenda. They predict that 6–8% of the general population might require special education even when practitioners in schools implement the components of an RTI framework with fidelity.

It is the role of the Tier 3 teacher to apply the most intense and specialized interventions that have been demonstrated effective when applied with children with reading disabilities. At each Tier 3 decision point (every 8 weeks), a problem-solving team (PST) should to meet to review the data and update the decision about the child's status. The PST should include the classroom teacher, Tier 3 teacher, special education teacher, school psychologist, and other personnel who work with the child. PST meetings need to discuss these children at each decision point to ensure that a "wait-to-fail" situation has not been created. Based on an evaluation of all data collected and recorded in the child's assessment portfolio, the PST will decide whether an in-depth evaluation by the school psychologist is in order.

Such an evaluation is the first step in the formal special education referral process. Special education is defined as "specialized instruction provided at no cost to the parents or guardians, to meet the unique needs of a child with a disability" (Individuals with Disabilities Education Improvement Act [IDEA] of 2004, Public Law No. 108-446, Part A, Sec. 602 [29]). Given 90 to 100 days of intense instruction, a child who still meets the dual-discrepancy criterion (low achievement and low rate of progress) is likely to require a formal evaluation to eliminate the possibility that the reading difficulty is the result of sensory impairment, intellectual disability, emotional disturbance, or environmental influences. As a result of IDEA 2004, the PST must not require the use of a severe IQ–achievement discrepancy for determining whether a child has a reading disability that qualifies him or her for the services and accommodations provided by special education! Today, many experts recommend replacing the IQ–achievement discrepancy criterion with the dual-discrepancy criterion (Burns, Christ, Boice, & Szadokierski, 2010; Fuchs et al., 2008; Hintze & Marcotte, 2010; McMaster et al., 2002).

Evaluating both the data from the psychologist's formal evaluation *and* the portfolio of data depicting the child's response to the scientific research-based interventions, the PST and the student's parents can decide what combination of special services are needed to best support the child's literacy achievement. In an RTI model, students are eligible for special education when the frequency, intensity, or duration of the intervention exceeds the resources available within general education (Burns et al., 2010). Some of these categories of support include, but are not limited to, long-term individualized intervention, standardized test accommodations, and in severe cases a comprehensive literacy program that is provided outside the general education context. Special education is the mechanism that has been designed and funded legislatively to meet these unique needs.

During the evaluation process, the child continues to receive Tier 3 intervention. If the PST decides that the child qualifies for the benefits of special education, a tiered model has the potential to make the transition seamless. In some schools, the special education teacher is the Tier 3 intervention provider. In other schools using an inclusion model, the special education teacher may be working with the child in the classroom.

Most of the instructional techniques applied during Tier 3 are based on research that was conducted with children with identified reading disabilities. This fact ensures a good alignment between the strategies Tier 3 teachers implement and those that will be used in a special education setting. Consequently, IEP goals are more likely to be based on the data collected during the prequalifying interventions and Tier 3 diagnostic process than to be derived from a short psychological measure given by a stranger within a short time frame (Brown-Chidsey, 2005; Burns et al., 2010; Fuchs et al., 2008). Special education must have the most intense level of instruction. It may involve further adjustments in duration, frequency, and group size that might enhance the effectiveness of instruction begun during Tier 3 (Fuchs et al., 2008). Within the special education setting, the perpetuation of a problem-solving model that makes use of data-driven, research-based practice needs to be applied as opposed to a canned, scripted program that is more suitable for a typical learner than a child with a severe reading disability who has been legally guaranteed an "*individualized* educational plan." Of course, progress monitoring continues and may be performed and evaluated more frequently than it was in Tier 3 to ensure that high expectations for the achievement of ambitious goals persist in the special education setting. In order for most schools to provide this quality of reading instruction, those teachers who will be working with the neediest students will require extensive, differentiated, and ongoing professional development.

THE DIAGNOSTIC PROCESS

The child who arrives in Tier 3 is a mystery waiting to be solved. The job of the Tier 3 teacher is to collect and interpret the diagnostic clues that will lead to effective instruction and accelerated reading achievement for the child facing an instructional crisis. This process begins with a collection of all existing data, including assessment results collected by the Tier 1 and, if applicable, the Tier 2 teacher. We will refer to this collection of test data as a portfolio, though our analogy is more like an investment portfolio than a collection of creative products or anecdotal notes. Like an investment portfolio, it will consist of the identified assets and liabilities that together make up the student's reading profile. This data portfolio will provide a starting point for determining the general area or areas of the child's difficulty. The diagnostic process is much less complicated for younger children than it is for older children. The process is also complicated when there are issues of linguistic diversity or a history of emotional-behavioral challenges. Utilization of the cognitive model (Figure 2.1; McKenna & Stahl, 2009) can provide a systematic way to identify a student's strengths and weaknesses. It provides a means for determining a child's continuum of mastery within each reading construct: skills mastered and consolidated, unconsolidated skills being used but frequently confused, skills under consideration, and skills on the horizon. The diagnosis of constrained skills (most foundational skills) can occur in a fairly linear fashion. However, the diagnosis of the unconstrained skills needs to consider that capability in these skills is likely to vary by text, genre, topic, and context. As a result, multiple assessments must be applied to gain a sense of a child's performance in a range of settings when determining abilities in the two broad areas of language comprehension and application of strategic knowledge.

Where to Begin

Based on the classroom teacher's estimate of instructional reading level, the Tier 3 teacher completes a full reading battery to determine independent, frustration, and possibly listening capacity levels. Either the school-adopted assessment kit or a commercially published informal reading inventory can be used to collect this information. Students in the intermediate grades need to be assessed reading both narrative and informational texts. Teachers must be vigilant in adhering to the assessment's administration procedures. In addition to reading levels, these tests provide a wealth of information. A full error analysis of oral reading in the early grades and a thorough analysis of the comprehension responses (both retelling and question answering) in the intermediate grades are crucial for informing teaching points. Additionally, the informal reading inventory data point the Tier 3 teacher to specific areas within the cognitive model that merit more in-depth diagnostic assessment.

For students in grade 3 and above, the TOWRE Tests of Phonemic Decoding Efficiency and Sight Word Efficiency provide normed guidelines for determining whether the older child's foundational skills are where they need to be (Torgesen et al., 1999). If children are performing poorly in these areas compared to other children in their age cohort, then specific diagnostics and instruction are warranted in the areas of decoding and high-frequency words. Because CBM screening tasks do not target these areas in the intermediate grades and older children may *appear* to know the foundational skills, the TOWRE quickly provides a lens for viewing not whether children know foundational skills but how their facility with these skills compares to their age (or grade-level) peers.

Christina was working with Rhianna, a sixth grader who was reading between 75 and 85 WCPM on grade-level texts, hovering around the 10th percentile rank in January (Hasbrouck & Tindal, 2006). Her instructional reading level was fifth grade, with a reading rate ranging from 95 to 100 WCPM, still ranking below the 25th percentile rank. Christina insisted that Rhianna knew the 300 most commonly occurring high-frequency words and was functioning at the syllable-affix stage of word-study development (Bear et al., 2011). Therefore, Christina was astounded when Rhianna's performance on the TOWRE Phonemic Decoding Efficiency test placed her at the 14th percentile rank and her Sight Word Efficiency score placed her at the 3rd percentile rank compared to other students her age. Based on these results, Christina proceeded to drill the trickier high-frequency words (those beginning with *wh-* and *th-* plus similar multisyllabic words like *county* and *country*). She also assessed Rhianna's automaticity with words at the next level of frequency (400–500 words) that still caused hesitation (Davies & Gardner, 2010).

Additionally, she implemented Topping's (1987) paired reading of sophisticated chapter books to provide high volumes of practice reading. Engaging in the duet (unison) reading with Christina during paired reading enabled Rhianna to encounter a higher volume of words than she would have encountered while reading texts at her instructional level or without assistance. Increased encounters with high-frequency words in connected text provided the repeated exposures needed for increasingly automatic recognition. Within 8 weeks, Rhianna's reading rate ranged from 135 to 140 WCPM on fifth-grade material and between 120 and 130 WCPM on sixth-grade material.

Diagnostics

Given the child's preliminary data, the Tier 3 teacher can identify the diagnostic assessments that will provide the lens for viewing the precise focus of instruction. Analyzing a child's performance using the cognitive model (Figure 2.1; McKenna

& Stahl, 2009) and the child's existing assessment data portfolio, the Tier 3 teacher determines which constructs are presenting hurdles to the child's reading progress. Based on the data collected by the classroom teacher (including screening data), the informal reading inventory, and the TOWRE (for older children), the pathway of primary concern is identified as falling within one of three main areas: (1) automatic word recognition, (2) language comprehension, or (3) strategic knowledge. Although a child can experience difficulties in more than one of these areas, we need to consider each one separately. Next, the appropriate diagnostic assessments based on each construct are selected to provide detailed clues about the child's reading process. See Figures 6.3 and 6.4.

In working with the youngest children, the developmental span is narrower so a broader view of teaching may be taken because there are fewer instructional gaps to fill than is the case with older readers. Diagnostics within the cognitive model's path of automatic word recognition are typically called for in order to target skill instruction. Often children at this stage have misunderstandings about how to apply and orchestrate the isolated skills into a cohesive process while reading and writing connected text. So it is imperative that the diagnostic process accounts for how this orchestrated practice will be incorporated into the Tier 3 intervention. Intervention models such as Reading Recovery (Clay, 2005), the interactive strategies approach (Scanlon et al., 2010), the comprehensive instructional model (Dorn & Henderson, 2010), and Reading Rescue (Ehri, Dreyer, Flugman, & Gross, 2007) are all intervention protocols that have been designed to accommodate these needs. Each provides a slightly different balance of isolated foundational skills and connected text

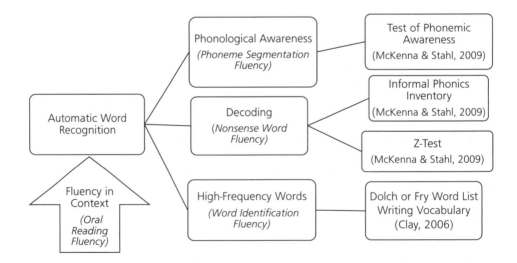

FIGURE 6.3. Diagnostic path for foundational skills and fluency.

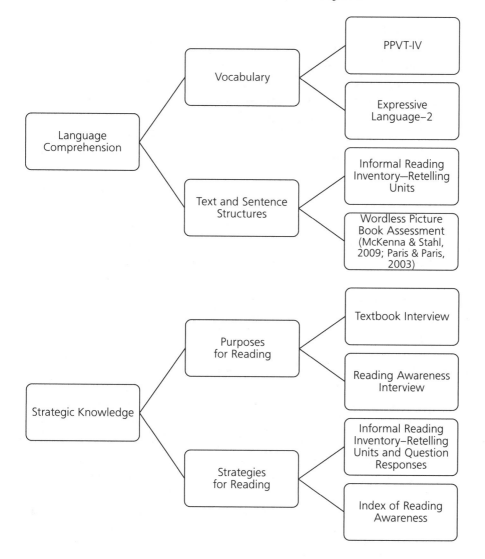

FIGURE 6.4. Diagnostic path for comprehension difficulties.

reading and writing, but they all share a common diagnostic approach and they effectively address the needs of the emergent-to-novice reader. Each intervention protocol uses diagnosis to target each child's skill development while providing rich opportunities for broader application in reading and writing connected text. Schools can find a range of research support for each protocol. In each Tier 3 session, time is devoted to teaching the particular isolated skills identified by the diagnostic assessments, but attention is also devoted to the application of the skills during reading and writing authentic, connected text.

Diagnosing and meeting the needs of the older reader is more of a challenge. Crafting a plan that addresses multiple needs requires that we balance priorities with available time. This balancing act is more easily accomplished for younger children than for those in the upper grades. Because silent reading, comprehending disciplinary content, and writing in response to text predominate the intermediate classroom, these are the proficiencies that must be assessed and incorporated in the diagnostic profile (McKenna & Stahl, 2009). Interviews that tap into students' perceptions about the purposes of reading and strategy application can provide insights into a student's challenges with comprehension. Some informal reading inventories also have passages formatted with think-alouds that are useful for assessing comprehension processes (Leslie & Caldwell, 2010).

Tier 3 teachers should also remember that the cognitive model is just that—*cognitive*. It is designed to detect deficiencies in the "thinking" side of reading. With older readers, however, gathering information about the affective dimensions of reading can also be useful. In addition to the difficulties posed by reading skills and strategies, affective challenges often interfere with reading achievement because of the cumulative influence of frustrating experiences. Diagnosis of needs must include measures of motivation, attitude, self-efficacy, and interests (McKenna & Stahl, 2009).

Once data have been gathered from the set of diagnostic assessments, tough decisions must be made. Unlike the Tier 3 interventions for the youngest readers, which are improved by breadth, the interventionist for the oldest readers must prioritize needs and find ways to provide depth in one or two key areas while providing tools of compensation and self-regulation for broader academic survival. Feelings of being overwhelmed with so many challenges must never be a call for surrendering Tier 3 to activities such as homework help or test-prep workshops. These children are in crisis and Band-Aids such as these are not worth the time or resource investment. These students must work with a reading expert who can instructionally target their most severe and fundamental reading needs while allocating time within the intervention to provide instruction in general classroom survival. Survival skills include strategies such as survey, question, read, recite, and review (SQ3R; Robinson, 1970) and self-regulated strategy development (De La Paz, Owen, Harris, & Graham, 2000; Graham & Harris, 1989, 2003).

For schools that are not accustomed to engaging in this form of diagnostic process, it might appear to be too time consuming. However, the time invested in diagnosis is valuable because it yields an instructional precision that is not otherwise possible. No instructional time is wasted teaching what the child already knows or what is beyond his or her ZPD. Combined with weekly progress monitoring, the diagnostic analysis situates children for ongoing reading achievement. It also allows for both quantitative and qualitative data collection over time that can comprehensively inform a potential evaluation for special education services and allow the child to make a smooth transition into special education.

PROGRESS MONITORING

Students in Tier 3 must have their ongoing progress monitored frequently. Because they are functioning far below their grade-level peers and the recipients of extensive school resources, every instructional session is crucial to an ascending learning trajectory. Foundational skills should be monitored weekly using CBM tasks. By now, it should go without saying that progress monitoring tasks should mirror the tasks that are screened at each grade level. Running records of text reading might be taken daily as primary-level children read books at their instructional level. Because older children will only be screened using the CBM maze, teachers of older students might use the number of idea units or story grammar units presented in an untimed oral retelling or the number of words in a timed written response to text as progress monitoring tasks. These kinds of tasks represent comprehension gains that are both quantifiable and also in alignment with the goals of most intermediate-level classrooms. Certainly, if the older student's target learning priority for an instructional round is still one of the foundational constructs, it would be the focus area of progress monitoring.

When intervention sessions are planned diagnostically, the progress monitoring aligns neatly with instruction. Therefore, allocating time for progress monitoring is not intrusive in Tier 3 because it mimics and simply replaces a similar instructional time slot. For example, if a child is working on summarizing text throughout the week, the same time slot is used on Friday for progress monitoring. What the child does during progress monitoring is unlikely to look very different from the practice during the other 4 days; the chief differences are that the teacher (1) does not provide scaffolding, and (2) formally documents the child's proficiency at a particular point in time. Additionally, the time allocation for the student progress monitoring activity is likely to be briefer and more precise.

OTHER TEST POSSIBILITIES

Because the children in their second or third round of Tier 3 instruction are likely candidates for referrals to special education, some reading specialists will administer the normed, standardized tests that are often associated with the referral process. Particularly, if the reading specialists have extensive training in a range of assessments or if there are specific tests that might inform Tier 3 instruction or the decision to refer, the Tier 3 teacher might administer some additional standardized tests. For example, a reading specialist might implement the PPVT-4 and the Expressive Vocabulary Test–2 to a student in second grade who reads fluently but has difficulty expressing comprehension of texts. Including some standardized tests in the student's assessment portfolio provides the school psychologist with a familiar frame of reference and may add weight to the referral for the comprehensive evaluation.

Machek and Nelson (2007) reported that most school psychologists believe that RTI and the use of a data portfolio reflecting a dual discrepancy are valid ways to define reading disability. However, in the same study over 60% of the school psychologists in the sample reported that they rarely used CBMs to make a decision about eligibility for special education. Instead, 78% of the psychologists indicated that they applied data that displayed intraindividual differences in cognitive processing and difficulties with phonological core processing, whereas 62% continued to endorse the IQ–achievement discrepancy model. Based on these results, it seems that teachers need to be armed with as much standardized data as possible when presenting their students' histories to the PST and the school psychologist.

THE DIAGNOSTIC PROCESS FOR A FIRST GRADER

Mac is a 6-year-old first grader who transferred to Metropolitan Elementary School after the winter holiday break. It is the fourth school that he has attended since he began kindergarten the previous school year. English is his first language. Based on his performance on the school's first-grade midyear screening tasks, he was identified as needing intensive literacy support (see Figure 6.5). He was functioning well below the grade-level performance benchmarks in isolated foundational skills (DIBELS Next) and oral reading of connected text. (The school's expectation was Fountas and Pinnell, 2006, Level F, compared with Mac's performance at Level B.) In light of the intensity of his needs, the PST decided to supplement his Tier 1 literacy instruction with 1:1 services in a Tier 3 setting. Ms. Chern, the literacy specialist, conducted additional diagnostic assessments in order to determine the best course of instruction.

Mac had not read any words on the DIBELS Next NWF task, but he had identified 10 correct letter sounds. Although this information alerted teachers that Mac was well below the first-grade benchmark, no analysis of 10 randomly identified sounds could be considered a reliable gauge of his knowledge about letter–sound relationships. A systematic and comprehensive analysis of his knowledge was called for, so Ms. Chern conducted the Informal Phonics Inventory (McKenna & Stahl, 2009). She compared his developmental performance in decoding to the encoding data that his classroom teacher had collected using the Words Their Way Elementary Spelling Inventory (Bear et al., 2011). Her data analysis indicated that Mac had no difficulties reading or spelling the beginning and ending sounds represented by a single consonant. He used but confused consonant digraphs and initial consonant blends in spelling but demonstrated mastery in reading, so a review was required. Both reading and spelling final blends were beyond his level of ability. Although he typically represented the middle of a word with a vowel approximation in his spelling, the short vowels were commonly confused in both decoding and encoding. Explicit, systematic instruction of all short vowels was warranted. Weekly tests

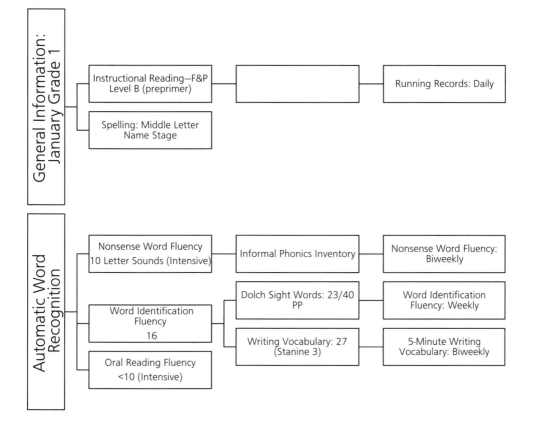

FIGURE 6.5. Mac's diagnostic directives for winter, round 1.

would be conducted to gauge mastery of each taught skill. Biweekly NWF progress monitoring would enable Ms. Chern to keep her eye on his progress toward the overarching goal of 58 letter sounds and 13 nonsense WPM by the end of the year. These assessment tasks are conducted during the phonics portion of the lesson so that there is minimal disruption to the lesson format. Figure 6.6 displays Mac's daily Tier 3 lesson agenda and his progress monitoring schedule.

During their assessment audit process, Metropolitan Elementary School made a commitment to teach children high-frequency words based on the Dolch List that has been divided into grade-level clusters (see McKenna & Stahl, 2009, pp. 123–124). Teachers in kindergarten are committed to teaching their children to read the high-frequency words on the preprimer list, first-grade teachers are accountable for teaching their students to automatically recognize the primer and first-grade list, and so on. Based on the consensus criterion of 1 second or less per word, Mac was able to identify only 23 of the 40 words on the preprimer list. His score on the word-identification fluency (WIF) task was 16. Since children are expected to recognize the words within 1 second, the performance goal is a score of 60. In constructing

3 minutes	High-frequency word writing *Every other Friday: 5-minute writing vocabulary progress monitoring*
5 minutes	Rereading familiar books (student-selected, previously read to teacher)
8 minutes	*Daily progress monitoring of oral reading text level*: running record book (briefly introduced and read once yesterday); no assistance provided during student reading (see Form 4.1)
5 minutes	Follow-up teaching/coaching based on Mac's reading, errors, self-corrections; attention to application of isolated skills and processing during reading of connected text
5–8 minutes	Sentence writing by Mac in response to teacher prompt related to the text
5 minutes	Explicit phonics instruction *Every other Friday: nonsense word fluency progress monitoring*
3 minutes	High-frequency word drill (reading) *Every Friday: word identification fluency progress monitoring*
8 minutes	Introduce new book; Mac reads it once with minimal assistance

FIGURE 6.6. Mac's daily Tier 3 intervention agenda.

their WIF CBMs using the Intervention Central website tool, the first-grade teachers created lists of 75 words that are a random assortment of the preprimer, primer, and first-grade Dolch words (*www.interventioncentral.org*). These lists are used for screening and progress monitoring. Ms. Chern will systematically conduct isolated drills on the preprimer word list before moving to the primer and first-grade lists as Mac's automatically recognized word bank increases. Progress monitoring using a random selection of words that need to be mastered by the end of first grade will be conducted each Friday during the portion of the lesson normally reserved for practicing high-frequency words. Using the Fuchs and Fuchs (2004) weekly growth rate formula, his progress monitoring end-of-year goal is 40 (1.5 WIF typical weekly growth rate × 16 weeks + Mac's 16 midyear baseline = 40) and his criterion goal is to automatically recognize 90% of the words on the preprimer, primer, and first-grade lists.

During Mac's Tier 3 intervention, Ms. Chern will also be supporting Mac's growing ability to write the high-frequency words automatically and correctly in every detail. By reading common words frequently in isolation and in connected texts, then using them in his own writing in connected text and reviewing them in isolation during the first few minutes of each lesson, his ability to write a collection of high-frequency words will improve. Clay's (2006) writing vocabulary task requires children to write as many words as possible within a 10-minute time frame. Mac was only able to write 27 words correctly placing him in the third stanine, or somewhat below the average. Metropolitan Elementary values the ability to write high-frequency words with automaticity. Therefore, when needed (as in Mac's case), Ms. Chern administers an abbreviated 5-minute writing vocabulary task biweekly as a means of progress monitoring. She will conduct this on alternate Fridays during the first 5 minutes of his lesson.

Mac's difficulties with the foundational skills are contributing to his difficulty reading connected text. Because Mac is new to the school, Ms. Chern and his classroom teacher, Mr. Fritz, have no way of knowing the contributing causes to Mac's current low performance levels. They do feel an urgent need to get books in his hands and to begin engaging him in reading a high volume of texts at his instructional level. Both teachers will be providing daily coaching as Mac becomes accountable for reading increasingly difficult books. Ms. Chern will take daily running records and chart the text levels and accuracy rates.

Based on Mac's low reading level and attention needed to build his foundational skills, she has decided not to progress-monitor his ORF (WCPM) using the DIBELS Next progress monitoring materials during the winter Round 1 intervention cycle. Instead, the PST will evaluate the most appropriate progress monitoring tools before Mac begins his second 8-week cycle, winter Round 2. At that point, the development of Mac's foundational reading skills and his instructional text level may indicate that using a grade-level ORF passage for progress monitoring is appropriate. However, based on Mac's midyear screening results, the PST deemed it inappropriate during winter Round 1.

THE DIAGNOSTIC PROCESS FOR A THIRD GRADER

Dino is a 9-year-old boy in third grade at Metropolitan Elementary School. He has attended Metropolitan Elementary since kindergarten entry. Screening measures and other assessments in the primary grades never indicated any severe reading problems for Dino. He functioned well on assessments of foundational skills. However, the increased emphasis on comprehension assessments and his school's transition to DIBELS Next pointed to some comprehension challenges in the beginning of third grade. He participated in a small-group standard protocol intervention during the fall that focused on fluency and comprehension. Minimal improvement was made during two rounds of Tier 2 instruction (see Figure 5.1). Additionally, both his classroom teacher and his mother were concerned about his deteriorating attitude toward all literacy activities. His mother reported that brief homework tasks often monopolized the better part of an evening and temper tantrums frequently accompanied writing assignments.

Data collected during the school's midyear screening confirmed the observations of Ms. Barilla (Dino's classroom teacher) and Dino's mother; Dino was encountering challenges comprehending grade-level texts despite his ability to read them fluently. Because two rounds (Fall 1 and Fall 2) of the standardized Tier 2 protocol had not helped Dino get on track, the PST recommended a transition to Tier 3. Ms. Chern gathered Dino's assessment portfolio and began the diagnostic process (see Figure 6.7).

Ms. Chern administered the TOWRE subtests to eliminate the possibility of any specific decoding issues and to confirm the strength of Dino's foundational abilities compared to his age peers. Dino's score on Sight Word Efficiency placed him at the 73rd percentile rank and his Phonemic Decoding score placed him at the 45th percentile rank. Dino achieved the benchmarks for rate and accuracy on the DIBELS Next ORF. However, he performed poorly on the ORF Retelling, DAZE,

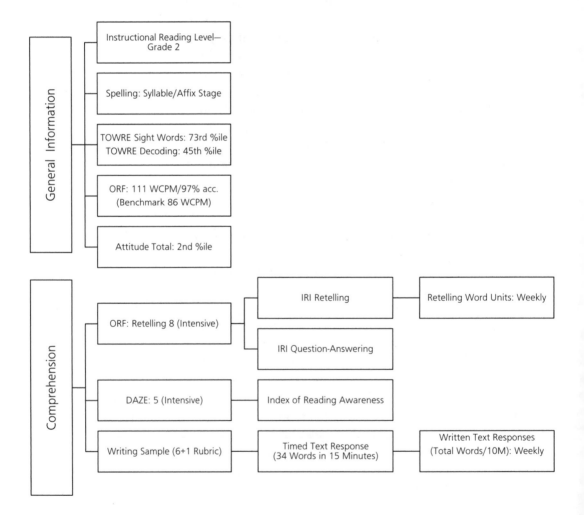

FIGURE 6.7. Dino's diagnostic directives for winter, round 1.

and the classroom informal reading inventory. Ms. Chern completed a comprehensive IRI to determine his independent and frustration levels, reading both narrative and informational texts. He was asked to retell each passage, answer explicit and implicit questions, and to create a written response to a text passage.

On the IRI, Dino was able to read second- and third-grade passages with high levels of accuracy (above 97%) and rate (124–153 WCPM). However, he was only able to provide a retelling of between 15 and 22% of the idea units for any of the passages, including an additional third-grade passage that Ms. Chern read to him. She used the additional passage to measure his listening comprehension. He tended to list a few isolated, random episodes or ideas using the precise wording of the text rather than paraphrasing the text passage and presenting key narrative story elements or the gist of the informational passages. In retelling the informational passages, he added tangential information from his experience while ignoring key elements from the passage. He correctly answered 50% of the questions following each second-grade passage; when prompted to look back, his score increased to 75% for the narrative and 88% correct for the informational text. Even with look-backs, he was unable to provide a correct response to more than 50% of the questions on any third-grade passage regardless of whether he read it or listened to it. Both explicit and implicit questions were answered incorrectly. Dino needed instruction that would help him utilize narrative and informational text structures, identify themes, and determine levels of importance. Ms. Chern decided that increasing the number of idea units in his retellings would provide the best measure of progress. Since Dino was able to read grade-level texts accurately, she decided to progress-monitor the number of idea units in his weekly retelling, using grade-level text passages provided on a website by their core reading series (see Figure 6.8).

The Index of Reading Awareness (Jacobs & Paris, 1987; McKenna & Stahl, 2009) provided Ms. Chern with information regarding Dino's approach to academic text with subtests that assessed text evaluation, planning, regulation, and

5 minutes	Explicit comprehension strategy lesson
10 minutes	Silent or oral reading of narrative or informational text; possible application of graphic organizer as temporary visual scaffold
5 minutes	Retelling and discussion of text *Every Friday: retelling progress monitoring (idea units)*
15 minutes	Self-regulated strategy development; written response to text *Every Friday: written response to text progress monitoring (words/10 minutes)*
10 minutes	Paired reading with questioning and discussion (see Topping, 1987)

FIGURE 6.8. Dino's daily Tier 3 intervention agenda.

conditional knowledge. An analysis of Dino's responses revealed that his most sig-nificant need was self-regulation. In combination with an evaluation of a writing sample that Dino completed in response to a teacher read-aloud, Ms. Chern deter-mined that it would be useful to apply two of the techniques that are components of self-regulated strategy development (SRSD; Graham & Harris, 1989, 2003; Harris, Graham, Mason, & Friedlander, 2008). In order to develop Dino's self-regulation in support of his reading and writing, she used S-P-A-C-E (setting, purpose, actions, conclusion, emotions) and POW: W-W-W-What2-How2 (Pick my idea, Organize my notes, Write and say more: Who is the main character? When does the story take place? Where does the story take place? What do the characters do? What hap-pens then? How does the story end? How do the characters feel?). These strategies provided consistency and depth to her reading and writing goals. Dino's baseline writing sample consisted of 34 words written in 15 minutes (Harris et al., 2008). Because Ms. Chern wanted her intervention experience to mimic what Dino would encounter at the end of the year on their statewide tests, her progress monitoring always followed the reading of a grade-level passage and the writing time limit was 10 minutes. She used total words written as the scoring unit (Hosp et al., 2007).

Ms. Chern's diagnostic evaluation revealed that Dino's negative attitude about literacy and a lack of motivation to read were among his most severe needs. Com-pared to other third graders, his attitude about recreational reading ranked in the bottom percentile. In other words, in a group of 100 third graders, 99 would be likely to possess a more positive attitude toward recreational reading than Dino. His attitude toward academic reading was slightly higher, in the 8th percentile rank. His composite ranking was in the 2nd percentile rank. This was extremely alarming considering the fact that attitudes tend to worsen as children get older.

Ms. Chern conducted an interest inventory to determine some ways that she could make the reading sessions engaging for Dino. She discovered that Dino enjoyed the Diary of a Wimpy Kid and Goosebumps book series. He also loved playing and watching baseball. In addition to finding texts about baseball and base-ball players, Ms. Chern created a writing incentive chart in the shape of a baseball diamond. During the daily lessons, Dino's written responses of 35 words earned a single, a 50-word response was a double, a 75-word response was a triple, and it took 100 words to score a home run. Similarly, Ms. Chern categorized questions as gold medal, silver medal, or bronze medal based on the level of conceptual dif-ficulty. During paired reading using complex chapter books, she increased engage-ment by having Dino answer and eventually generate a range of questions requiring different levels of thought (Topping, 1987). Ms. Chern was deliberate in selecting challenging texts about Dino's interests or multiple theme-related texts were read across an entire week to build knowledge and interest. For example, when Dino's class was studying a science unit on plants, he read texts and wrote about carnivo-rous plants, the world's strangest plants, and the world's most amazing plants during his Tier 3 intervention.

WHAT HAPPENS NEXT WHEN TIER 3 WORKS?

For Mac and Dino, these stories had a happy ending. The Tier 3 intervention was exactly what was needed to get them back on track. At the end of each 8-week round of instruction the PST reviewed the progress monitoring charts for the Tier 3 students. Both boys stayed in Tier 3 for two rounds of instruction. At the end-of-year screening, Dino achieved reading benchmarks. Additionally, on the state English language arts test he scored within the proficient range. Based on a triangulation of multiple consistent data sources, the PST recommended that unless there were severe dips in his fourth-grade beginning-of-the-year assessments, Dino should start fourth grade receiving Tier 1 instruction with biweekly progress monitoring during differentiated instruction. Because the PST was familiar with his case, the school-level PST members (Ms. Chern, the special education teacher, and the school psychologist) would put him on a "watch" list for the following fall. Being placed on the "watch" list ensured that Dino would be monitored closely by the PST for one or two rounds of instruction following the Tier 3 intervention.

Mac made excellent progress. Although he exceeded his WIF goal and achieved the grade-level performance benchmark for NWF, his text reading level (Fountas & Pinnell, 2006, Level F) was considered to be only "approaching grade level" at Metropolitan Elementary. Additionally, at the end of the school year he was still well below benchmark on the ORF. For planning purposes, the PST made a tentative recommendation to provide Tier 2 services to Mac during the fall of second grade, focusing on fluency. Naturally, more conclusive determinations would be made based on the beginning-of-the-year screening tasks. However, the good news at the end of first grade was that Mac had made accelerated progress and at this point in time he was not a candidate for referral for special education.

These scenarios illustrate a few of the roles of the PST. In addition to working with the classroom teachers to make decisions about possible interventions for children, the PST serves as a consistent advocate for children with the most severe reading problems as they move from grade level to grade level and between settings. The PST guarantees that children are not falling between the cracks, yo-yoing between tiers for multiple years, or starting new prereferral interventions every September. The PST ensures that the momentum that was begun in a Tier 3 setting in 1 year is continued at the beginning of the following year with as much service as needed for the child to continue an uninterrupted, ascending trajectory. Likewise, given the exemplary data-driven research-based instruction that has been described, a child who ends the year with a dual discrepancy is entitled to a formal evaluation to complete the diagnostic process and to an assurance that everything possible is being done by the school to promote his or her academic achievement.

The exception to this guideline is when the student is an EL. Evidence indicates that many ELs require extended rounds of tiered intervention to achieve grade-level benchmarks (Linan-Thompson et al., 2006; Orosco & Klingner, 2010).

While ELs in the primary grades may achieve the most constrained skills relatively quickly, the ability to apply word-attack skills to connected text, comprehend text, and express that comprehension using both oral and written expression develop more slowly (K. A. D. Stahl & Keane, 2010; K. A. D. Stahl, Keane, & Simic, in press). Therefore, a more liberal attitude regarding the number of intervention rounds needs to be considered prior to referral. The use of progress monitoring to demonstrate ongoing growth is useful for guiding the instructional decision making that is central to this process.

CHAPTER SEVEN

Communicating Assessment Outcomes

G athering assessment data is an empty exercise if the data are not used to make decisions that benefit children. So far, we have examined the uses of data to plan appropriate instruction at each tier. This examination is a bit like placing a child under a magnifying glass to get a better idea of immediate needs. A magnifying glass is, to be sure, a useful tool for inspecting the near-term progress of children. When that examination is guided by the cognitive model, we are in a position to reach preliminary conclusions about the instruction that is most likely to be effective and to test those conclusions through day-to-day interactions with the child. Extending our metaphor, we now consider a different kind of lens, one that is equally useful in guiding our decisions by bringing the long-term picture of the child into focus. It is a wide-angle lens and it enables us to see learning trajectories more clearly over longer time spans and to make high-stakes decisions on the basis of reliable data that have been collected and stored with care.

SETTING UP A RECORD-KEEPING SYSTEM

Conducting an assessment at a single point in time can take us only so far in meeting a child's needs. No matter how thorough, such an assessment is of limited value in making predictions about future progress. It is like viewing a snapshot and trying to infer what might happen next. RTI is about changes that occur over time, and although snapshots do have their uses, we also need a "video" to help us understand a child's movement over the course of weeks and months. To capture such movement, we must have data gathered at different times. Just as important, we need a system that allows us to record such data conveniently and efficiently, to access it easily, and to use it to answer questions that pertain to the tough decisions we must make.

Unfortunately, there are no one-size-fits-all data storage systems. This is because any system depends on which assessments are given, and these vary widely. Screening batteries, such as AIMSweb, DIBELS Next, or PALS, have remote storage options but these may offer more than we need. Consequently, our best option may be to store RTI data in a system tailored to the assessments actually administered at each grade level.

Crafting a workable system is not as difficult as it may sound. We offer here some straightforward suggestions and a basic example of how such a system might look.

• *Use print and digital systems in tandem.* The choice between paper and digital records should not be either/or. Each has advantages the other lacks and together they can help answer the central questions about a child or groups of children. There is obvious appeal in a low-tech data notebook. Information can be browsed easily and without technology, and it can accommodate work samples and other documents. On the other hand, notebooks can become voluminous and hard to navigate. In addition, using them to produce summaries, pre–post comparisons, and other reports can be prohibitively time consuming. A notebook can back up an electronic system and house materials that may be of use in making important decisions about a child. Although print materials can be scanned and stored as PDF files, thereby enabling a school to go completely electronic, we see little reason to spend time doing so. The real value of a digital database lies in the ability to generate reports, both for individuals and groups, and to address specific questions about responsiveness.

• *Be selective.* More information is not always better. This is especially true for print documents, such as student work samples and assessment forms. It takes time and energy to interpret such documents, and we believe that a few can go a long way. For example, a longitudinal graph depicting weekly progress monitoring fluency scores is easy to interpret. In contrast, a series of running records is far more time consuming, and a few representative examples with a history of text-level growth displayed on a graph will usually suffice to give us an idea of trends.

Some schools that we work with have used some simple summary sheets at crucial points of the RTI decision-making process. See Form 7.1 and Form 7.2 at the end of this chapter. The Student Action Form (Form 7.1) may be used by PSTs to summarize the decision-making process for students who are being considered for or who have received interventions beyond Tier 1. This form is completed at each decision-making juncture. One copy is kept in the student's portfolio and the literacy coach or PST facilitator maintains one copy (paper or electronic) to document the interventions and the progress of each student in Tier 2 and Tier 3. The Summary

Sheet of Tiered Support (Form 7.2) can be used to synthesize all of the information from a series of Student Action Forms if a student is being recommended for evaluation to determine special education eligibility. It traces a student's history of tiered interventions and progress monitoring data on a single sheet.

• *Limit the digital component to screening and progress monitoring.* The principal use of the digital database is to periodically gauge responsiveness. Each column should help to shed light on this issue. If the data entered are not used for this purpose, it is hard to justify the time required to enter them or to regard them as little more than clutter. For example, consider Sam, a third grader at Metropolitan Elementary. Sam is screened in the fall and scores well below the ORF benchmark. Following the cognitive model, the teacher administers a high-frequency word inventory. Sam scores poorly and the teacher concludes that automatic recognition of more high-frequency words should be a target of Tier 1 differentiated instruction. Should the results of this inventory be entered into the digital database? We believe the answer depends on two considerations: (1) whether the teacher plans to readminister the inventory later so that a pre–post comparison is possible, and (2) whether there are other children with the same need. If Sam is a relative outlier among third graders at Metropolitan, it makes little sense to devote two columns in the database to these scores. This doesn't mean they aren't important, of course, but recording the inventory scores in print form will be adequate.

• *Set up a separate system for each grade level.* The assessments at each grade, particularly at the primary level, vary considerably, and so should the record keeping. In addition, although it may seem desirable to track individual struggling children from one grade to the next, it is difficult to construct an electronic system that is truly conducive to such tracking. Looking across grades is easy enough without creating a single massive database that includes all of the students in a school. Even when the goal is to generate the reports needed for a state-of-the-school address, we see little need for a multigrade data system.

• *Involve classroom teachers.* In Chapter 3, we identified individuals who are in the best position to administer and score each type of assessment in an RTI program. Classroom teachers play a role by giving informal assessments that are useful in day-to-day planning, but they do not typically administer the assessments used by teachers at Tiers 2 and 3. This does not mean, however, that they cannot benefit from knowing the results of these assessments. It is a good idea for specialists to touch base with classroom teachers—if only on the fly—to apprise them of developments concerning the children for whom they share responsibility. These conversations should be two-way as well. What the classroom teacher learns from informal assessments and day-to-day interactions can help clarify a child's needs for a specialist.

A single specialist or coach with responsibility for managing an RTI plan cannot realistically be expected to compile daily data on every student who exhibits difficulties. Classroom teachers must take on the role of administering progress monitoring assessments and recording them in way that allows the specialist to examine them periodically. Doing so not only distributes the workload but invests the classroom teacher more directly in the progress of individual children. These records can have a print or digital format. For example, a second-grade classroom teacher might record weekly fluency scores on a paper chart, and the specialist could enter scores at the end of 3- or 4-week intervals into an electronic database. The key is for everyone to have a clear idea of his or her expectations and then to follow through.

• *Make formative changes.* Both the print and digital components of a data system should be viewed as works in progress. Opportunities to make improvements will inevitably arise when we occasionally ask the following two questions (each of which is the flip side of the other):

1. Do we regularly need information that our records don't provide?
2. Are we keeping records that are rarely if ever used in decision making?

The answers to these questions should guide refinements in the RTI record-keeping system. The goal should be to include everything necessary and nothing more.

Figure 7.1 depicts the structure of a digital record-keeping database for third grade. The fact that it is generic does not mean that it will work for any school. The particular characteristics of the assessments selected and the frequency of administering them, together with other considerations, must be taken into account. For this example, we have used the DIBELS Next fall benchmark of 70 WCPM along with the cut point for risk of 55 to determine the risk levels, which are coded 1 (low), 2 (moderate), and 3 (high). These numbers could be computed automatically from the WCPM score by inserting formulas into the fourth column. If this structure were used to develop an Excel spreadsheet, it would be fairly simple to generate reports for Sam, for Ms. Smith's overall class profile, and for third grade as a whole.

Teacher	Student	Fall							Winter . . .
		BM/CP 70/55	Risk	3 weeks	6 weeks	9 weeks	12 weeks	15 weeks	BM/CP 86/68
Smith	Sam	50	3						
Smith	Latoya	74	1						
Smith	Fred	62	2						
. . .									

FIGURE 7.1. Example of an electronic database for third grade. BM/CP, benchmark/cut point for risk.

There are a number of important points to make about this example. First, not all of the screening assessments are necessarily represented. If Metropolitan Elementary universally administers a conventional IRI at third grade, for example, or a computer-adaptive comprehension measure such as the Scholastic Reading Inventory, these results would be included. Note next that there will be many empty cells in such a system. Latoya, for instance, is above the fall benchmark and her oral fluency will not be assessed again until winter benchmarking. Note also that Ms. Smith might well administer progress monitoring assessments every week, but she will record these scores on a graph rather than uploading them to the database. Remember too that she has decided to focus on high-frequency words. Readministering the high-frequency word inventory will be important in determining the immediate impact of her instruction, but these scores are not entered into the database because only one or two of her students will receive this instructional focus. Besides, the real test of Sam's responsiveness will be his improvement on the ORF subtest. Finally, the third-grade database is simple compared with its kindergarten or first-grade counterpart. This is because more benchmark assessments are given and because Metropolitan Elementary has decided to keep track of a variety of foundational skills, such as the number of letters a child can recognize, in order to better track students and evaluate its program.

ESTABLISHING DECISION POINTS FOR MOVING ACROSS TIERS

The role of assessments in RTI is never more apparent than when we make the crucial decision about whether to move a child from one tier to the next. We have depicted the indispensible role of assessment data in Figure 7.2. Although the type of data needed at each decision point is different, it is clear that the results of assessments enable us to gauge a child's RTI. They form the fuel that drives the RTI system at all points.

Expert opinion differs concerning decisions about whether a child is responding acceptably to an intervention. One view is that either three or four consecutive data points below the goal line warrant reconsideration of the approaches used (AIMSweb; Hosp et al., 2007). Walpole and McKenna (2007) recommend assessing after 3-week intervals for Tier 1 differentiated instruction (the approach reflected in Figure 7.1), although 3-week intervals could be used at any tier. The logic of repeated assessments is borrowed from an approach to research known as the single-subject experiment (see Neuman, 2011). Several periodic measurements are first taken to establish a student's baseline performance level. When the intervention begins, the assessments continue and are used to determine whether the intervention is resulting in improved performance. Multiple measurements at equal intervals are key to linking the intervention with achievement gains. They help a researcher "discern a clear pattern of consistency in the behavior over time" (Neuman, 2011, p. 385). In

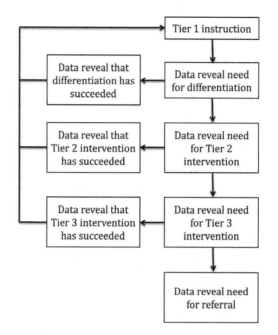

FIGURE 7.2. Using data at multiple points in an RTI system.

a very real sense, a teacher at any tier of an RTI model is conducting single-subject research into the effectiveness of an approach or program *for a particular child*. Of course, the teacher's efforts differ from the controlled environment of a research study. For example, there is no time to collect data at multiple points before an intervention begins. The situation is too urgent for that. Nor is there the luxury of altering just one variable at a time. Nevertheless, the logic is similar and we recommend Neuman's excellent chapter as a possible selection for a study group.

The main difference in the assessments used to determine a child's responsiveness to an intervention lies in how frequently they are administered (Hosp et al., 2007). A rule of thumb is that the more intensive the intervention, the more frequent the progress monitoring. What we feel is a consensus view appears in Table 7.1, although the actual frequency of progress monitoring assessment will be

TABLE 7.1. Frequency of Progress Monitoring Assessments by Tier

Tier	Frequency of progress monitoring
1 (differentiated instruction)	Every 3–4 weeks
2 (intervention)	Every 1–2 weeks
3 (intensive intervention)	One to two times per week

determined by the school's RTI framework, the interventionists working within each tier, and PST recommendations for specific children.

Assessment data can be used to guide a series of decisions about next steps for a child. Two questions have become central in RTI:

1. What is the child's level of performance?
2. Is the child making an acceptable rate of improvement?

The answer to the first question comes from comparing a child's scores to a norm or performance benchmark. The answer to the second comes from graphing the rate of progress and comparing it with the aim line. If the answer to both questions is yes, we are justified in concluding that the intervention is working. However, if no appreciable progress has been made or if the rate of progress is too slow, we must decide how to alter the instruction the child receives in a manner likely to be effective. This decision will involve making changes at the current tier or moving the child to a more intensive tier. Discussions should center around four basic issues (e.g., Mellard et al., 2010), and we have distilled them into these guiding questions:

1. Have the current instructional techniques been used frequently enough to have the intended effect?
2. Have they been in place long enough to make a measurable difference?
3. Are there alternative techniques that might produce better results?
4. Is the size of the group too large for the child to receive optimal benefits?

Discussions that address these questions may lead to decisions that involve changing the approach, increasing its frequency, extending its duration, or reducing group size. Some of these decisions may well require that a child proceed to a higher tier.

At each decision point, two critical factors should be considered. One is the availability of viable instructional alternatives. These may be either research-based techniques or commercial programs. For a *technique* to be available, it must have an adequate grounding in scientifically based research *and* the teacher must be able to apply it. For a *program* to be available, a third consideration is cost.

The second factor is whether the instruction provided has been delivered in the appropriate manner. In our experience, this factor is rarely addressed in RTI. Albers, Elliott, Kettler, and Roach (2005) have suggested that the decision of whether or not a child has responded to instruction must rest on two considerations. The first is whether the instruction provided was well matched to a child's needs (treatment acceptability); the second is whether the instruction was provided accurately (treatment fidelity). Sanetti and Kratochwill (2005) have commented that "An effective but poorly implemented intervention could be considered ineffective as a result of modifications in implementation" (p. 306). They point out that implementing an intervention with fidelity can be threatened by a teacher's motivation to implement it. For example, the teacher may not believe the approach will work and may therefore not implement it with fidelity. The teacher may alter the intervention in what is perceived as the child's best interest. If the results are unfavorable, the natural conclusion of the PST is likely to be that the intervention is to blame. To avoid such an unwarranted conclusion, it is important to determine whether the intervention was delivered accurately. Sanetti and Kratochwill suggest that teacher-reported checklists and observations by a coach (preferably both) can be useful in making this determination. In both cases, it is vital to define the intervention clearly, dividing it into specific components. In this way, a teacher will be able to respond to specifics about implementation, and a coach will have explicit guidance about what to look for during an observation.

If it is determined that a teacher has not provided an intervention in the prescribed manner, it is unfair to conclude that the child has not responded *to the intervention*. Needless to say, if such a case occurs at Tier 3, referral for special education is unwarranted. And of course, the same reasoning applies at Tiers 1 and 2 regarding the decision to attempt a more intensive intervention. When a low level of fidelity is suspected, the choice is between making a second attempt and monitoring for better fidelity or trying a different intervention at the same tier.

Taken together, these decisions form the blueprint of an RTI plan, and they are complex. To help organize the process, we have distilled them into the question-and-answer chart appearing in Figure 7.3. The questions progress systematically across tiers until the point of referral for special education is reached.

COMMUNICATING WITH TEACHERS

Although assessment data may be the fuel of an RTI system, the engine that burns that fuel is collaboration. Collecting data is an empty exercise if it is not part of a shared decision-making process. The difficulty lies in getting busy professionals together for the time required to make the decisions crucial to the learning trajectory of each struggling student. The suggestions that follow may make scheduling productive meetings easier.

• *Set up a regular schedule.* We have mentioned the need to meet at least every 8 weeks to make decisions about moving individual students across tiers or on to the referral stage. These decisions involve all of the children in the school, not only those who struggle. We need to be sure, for example, that those children who have met or exceeded performance benchmarks in the past are not beginning to experience problems. Naturally, additional time will be needed to consider students at risk, but every child should be on the radar. If enough time is set aside, perhaps a

Question	Answer
How do I tell which students are at risk?	Refer to benchmarks for the screening CBMs.
How do I determine instructional targets for children at risk?	Use the cognitive model to decide which diagnostics to administer.
How do I group children with similar instructional targets for Tier 1 differentiated instruction?	Use a combination of screening and diagnostic assessments to sort the children for best fit, understanding that compromises may be necessary.
How do I set reasonable instructional goals for Tier 1 small-group instruction?	Create aim lines based on CBM benchmarks.
How do I know when Tier 2 instruction is needed?	Decide whether Tier 1 differentiation has been adequately applied over the course of 3–4 weeks. If so, decide if there are available alternatives that appear viable at Tier 1.
How do I know when Tier 3 instruction is needed?	Decide whether Tier 2 intervention has been adequately applied over the course of 8 weeks. If so, decide if there are available alternatives that appear viable at Tier 2.
How do I know when a special education referral is appropriate?	Decide whether Tier 3 intervention has been adequately applied over the course of 8 weeks. If so, decide if there are available alternatives that appear viable at Tier 3.

FIGURE 7.3. Quick guide to making key decisions in RTI.

half or full day, a number of children can be considered in succession. Reserving this much time is obviously problematic, which leads to our next suggestion.

• *Seek administrative support.* The principal is in a position to facilitate periodic PST meetings, even those lasting a full day. The principal may be able to take certain actions that allow the PST to meet as needed. These include:

1. Paying extended-day stipends.
2. Arranging for coverage (assuming a qualified specialist is available).
3. Excusing team members from other activities, such as assemblies and professional development that is only remotely relevant.
4. Making RTI meetings a priority during the entire week after each screening period.

At one of the schools in which we work, this last option has worked extremely well. Schedules are adjusted to accommodate the meetings. Each teacher is allocated a 30-minute block to meet with the PST. The literacy coach leads the data discussion, and in-depth conversations address the progress and needs of the children who are not meeting the grade-level benchmarks. This is an opportunity for all of the teachers who work with a child to meet together at the same time and place. The Student Action Plan (Form 7.1) provides structure for a conversation about each at-risk student.

• *Schedule a common time.* The principal can help in one additional way before the year even begins. By scheduling a common planning time for PST members, the principal can enable them to meet on an as-needed basis throughout the year. The team will still need to schedule meetings, but a great logistical barrier will have been lifted.

• *Provide briefs to team members.* Starting from scratch with each student to be evaluated takes time. The PST leader, generally a coach or specialist, can shorten meeting times by generating reports, summarizing a child's history in bulleted fashion, and listing key issues to be considered. These can be read in advance by team members and become talking points at the meeting. We do not believe that this task really adds to the team leader's burden because these preparations will need to be made in any case.

• *Assemble all materials likely to be needed.* Additional time savings can result from having everything at your fingertips once the meeting starts. Beyond the database and reports the leader has generated, data notebooks and work samples may be useful.

• *Try meeting in cyberspace.* To be clear, we are not referring to virtual, real-time conferencing made possible through telecommunications. That requires that individuals be available at the same time, and because all are available in one school, a face-to-face meeting would be possible. However, when schedules conflict—when one member is available from 10:00 to 10:30, another from 10:30 to 11:00, and so on—an asynchronous meeting may be possible. This is accomplished by setting up blogs on a secure site. We recommend a unique blog or thread for each student. The team leader posts a summary of information and issues and the other team members react to it when they can. We realize that many educators may view such a "meeting" as a decidedly inferior option to a real sit-down. We see it as worth a try, however, and suggest two additional benefits as well. First, blogs create an ongoing record of team input documented by date. It is easy to review a student's history simply by reading through the blog from the beginning. Second, teachers other than PST members can participate, such as a special educator, the principal, or the classroom teacher.

COMMUNICATING WITH PARENTS

Being the parent of a child who struggles in school is not an enjoyable task. Communications from teachers rarely bring good news and it is easy to fall into a pattern of avoidance. Because parents have the potential to partner with teachers in the effort to assist their children, it is important that teachers reach out to them. Understanding the problems associated with this effort is important because it may suggest effective strategies for connecting with parents.

Paratore, Steiner, and Dougherty (2012) summarize the major hurdles in forging strong home–school relationships. One involves differences between parents and teachers on the matter of how their roles are perceived. Many teachers have been reared in middle-class homes where parents complement the work of teachers by supporting their children with assignments, reading to them, consciously assisting them with language development, and so forth. This support is very much a part of nearly any teacher's schema for what a parent should be.

When it becomes evident that the parents of their most challenging students do not provide this level of support, it is easy to blame these parents for neglecting their responsibilities and even for not caring enough about their children. We believe that this judgment is misguided. Many working-class parents make a clear-cut distinction between the proper role of home and school. They work long hours at low-paying jobs to provide for their children, while the job of the teacher is to educate those children. "Don't ask us to do your job," they often argue. There is also another well-documented reason for parents' reluctance to take a participatory role in assisting their children. Their avoidance is often rooted in a fear of school as an institution. It may well be a place that parents themselves associate with failure and frustration. In this regard, communicating with the school may also remind some parents of their limited self-efficacy. That is, they may feel they lack the know-how and resources to assist their children. Yet another difficulty, and one that is rapidly growing, arises when the language spoken at home is not English. Finally, the logistical issues of getting messages to economically disadvantaged parents who may move frequently and have limited access to telephones can be daunting.

We acknowledge that some of these barriers may prohibit reaching out successfully to some parents. However, we offer some suggestions that other teachers have found helpful and that may increase the number of parents you can ultimately serve.

- *Start with a clear agenda.* Decide on the message you wish to convey, including what, if anything, you will ask parents to do. Have all the documents you will need (student work, teacher notations, score reports, etc.) organized and ready.

- *Keep trying.* Don't give up when your initial efforts to reach parents fail. Failure to respond to requests doesn't mean they don't care.

- *Use multiple avenues to reach out.* Be resourceful. Pin notes to jackets, leave messages at work, ask other parents to convey messages. (And see previous suggestion.)

- *Put them at ease.* When you do make contact, work to make parents comfortable in a setting they may find intimidating. Meet with them in a sheltered location—an empty office, conference room, or classroom—away from ambient noise and student traffic.

- *Be mindful of language differences.* When a parent's first language is not English, discussions may be subject to misinterpretation and perhaps to the illusion that you have gotten your point across just because you made it. If you suspect that spoken English is a limitation, arrange for a bilingual teacher, aide, or volunteer to be present.

- *Accentuate the positive.* Good things can be said about the most challenging child, and every conversation should begin with those points.

- *Avoid jargon.* Limited English proficiency is not the only barrier to effective communication. As educators, we swim in a sea of terms and acronyms that can make discussions with noneducators dicey. Assume limited background knowledge, be clear, and use everyday language. You can be professional without being erudite. Your goal is to communicate, not to impress. Pause often and check (subtly) for understanding.

- *Avoid data overload.* Through RTI, concepts such as percentile ranks, benchmark scores, aim lines, data banks, tiers, and risk levels have become second nature. However, parents may need careful scaffolding if these ideas are to be understood. We believe, however, that very few references to such terms are needed. It is easy to fall into the trap of presenting parents with graphs and statistics and simply assuming that these tools are easy for anyone to interpret. They aren't! Look for other, clearer ways to summarize their child's growth.

- *Listen.* Although your main goal may be to inform parents of how their child is performing, they are an invaluable source of information that might shed light on a challenging child. By asking questions, you not only tap this information but engage the parents more fully in the act of problem solving. You can give the conference the look and feel of a conversation among concerned adults instead of a lecture.

- *Document your meeting in writing.* Conversations are easily forgotten, or remembered imperfectly. If you document a conference with a quick list of points in closing, you give the parents something to take with them (perhaps in two languages). At the same time you have created a documentation of those points. Of course, if you are unable to bring the parents in for a face-to-face meeting, a written document may constitute the only means of communication. This option is a distant second in terms of desirability, however. You have little way of knowing whether such a document was received, much less understood.

THE WHOLE TRUTH AND NOTHING BUT THE TRUTH: COMMUNICATING IN WAYS THAT MATTER

RTI produces an abundance of information, perhaps to a degree unparalleled in past initiatives. In this chapter we have examined a few of the ways in which that information can be shared in an effort to ground important decisions and to include parents as stakeholders. This would be all to the good were it not for two difficulties.

We worry, on the one hand, about adequate access to the information collected about children by all of the teachers who need it. To ensure such access, the RTI plan includes channels of communication that link educators who traditionally have not had a history of working closely together. Collaborating for RTI will no doubt be novel to teachers used to a "silo" mentality ("I'll do my job, you do yours"). This perspective is unacceptable in RTI, but we are concerned that some teachers will revert to form if the channels of communication are not kept open. We believe that the coach and principal are the two individuals best positioned to ensure that using these channels—regularly and in the manner intended—becomes standard operating procedure for a school. The "whole truth" should be accessible to all.

On the other hand, we also worry about information overload. Teachers suddenly awash in data may be perplexed and overwhelmed. In our experience, conversations designed to interpret data can become divergent and chatty, adding still more information, some of which may be irrelevant. Unless discussion leaders can maintain a clear focus and agenda, minutes will be lost, eyes will glaze over, and teachers will leave thinking they've wasted their time. It is important to remember that the "whole truth" must always be available but that it isn't always necessary.

Student Action Form

Date:

Student Name:	Birthdate:
Classroom Teacher:	Grade Level:

DECISION TEAM MEMBERS PRESENT:

_____Classroom Teacher   _____Administrator

_____Reading Specialist   _____Speech/Language Pathologist

_____Literacy Coach   _____Psychologist

_____Special Education Teacher   _____Other

_____Parent Notification   Date:

Intervention Plan for Tier _____
Instructional Text Reading Level _____
Primary areas of literacy difficulty/focus of intervention:
_____Phonological awareness   _____Comprehension
_____Phonics   _____Other (Provide description)
_____Fluency

Evidence of Difficulty (Performance data):

Instructional Recommendations:

(cont.)

Evidence to Demonstrate Progress

Assessments	Dates	Person responsible for data collection

Duration: _____ **Next Meeting Date:** _____

Performance Results:

Next Steps:

_____ Continue with prescribed intervention

_____ Develop a new plan for student to receive in this tier

_____ Tier 1 only with differentiation and increased progress monitoring

_____ Move to Tier 2

_____ Move to Tier 3

_____ Initiate referral to special education

Summary Sheet of Tiered Support

This sheet summarizes the instructional interventions that preceded a special education referral for a suspected learning disability that affects reading.

Student Name:	Birthdate:
Classroom Teacher:	Grade Level:

CORE GENERAL EDUCATION LANGUAGE ARTS INSTRUCTION (TIER 1)

☐ Student has participated in a minimum of 90 minutes of daily general education literacy instruction using scientific research-based practices provided to the entire class by the general education teacher.

Description of instruction provided:

SMALL GROUP/DIFFERENTIATED INSTRUCTION
BY GENERAL EDUCATION TEACHER (TIER 1)

☐ Student participated in differentiated instruction by the classroom teacher using materials at the student's instructional reading level and/or to provide additional support in a particular skill area.

Description of instruction provided:

(cont.)

Supplemental interventions (Tier 2, targeted intervention; Tier 3, more targeted and intensive intervention)

Tier	Instructional intervention	Dates	Provider

Sources of Evidence: Complete the table below *and* attach screening data indicating risk status and progress monitoring (including data in graphic formats).

Tier	Dates	Screen data and score	Intervention	Response to intervention (Baseline plus at least *four* additional progress monitoring measurements for each intervention)	

OTHER SOURCES OF EVIDENCE:

CHAPTER EIGHT

Creating an Effective RTI System

STAGING THE IMPLEMENTATION
OF AN EFFECTIVE RTI ASSESSMENT SYSTEM

For most schools, RTI represents a major change in the way education is planned and carried out. Such changes do not occur overnight and they do not always involve smooth sailing. In fact, classroom teachers and specialists will inevitably face some turbulence as routines are disrupted, roles are redefined, and existing beliefs are challenged. The key is having a steady hand on the tiller and a clear idea of where the school is headed.

In this book, we have examined the components of an RTI assessment system, one by one. It is time to put the pieces together. If your school has an RTI framework with a comprehensive assessment system in place, we hope this chapter serves as the basis for constructive contrasts. Think about where your present system is different and whether the differences might suggest possible changes. Consider how each component could be implemented and how the realities of policies and politics might help or hinder your efforts.

Let's review the three fundamental assumptions that underlie RTI:

1. Some instructional approaches work better than others.
2. Assessments can tell us how well they work for particular children.
3. Records of what has been tried over time are essential.

We can easily translate these assumptions into a to-do list for crafting an effective RTI system. First, we must decide which instructional approaches to endorse. Then we must choose assessments that are capable of gauging the impact of those approaches on the learning of individual children. Next, we must set up a simple but effective record-keeping system, one that permits us to track individuals, classrooms, and grade levels over the course of a year and enables easy communication across instructional tiers. Finally, we must plan professional development in a systematic way so that teachers are sufficiently knowledgeable about each component and so that expectations are clear.

SELECTING APPROACHES MOST LIKELY TO BE EFFECTIVE

In recommending the standard protocol for Tier 2, we acknowledge the importance of deciding which instructional approaches should be *standard*. One choice is to create an extensive menu of approaches. Teacher input could be solicited and professional judgment respected. Although these are appealing features in a change process, there are serious problems with this plan. One is that teachers can be expected to identify their favorite approaches, those with which they are most comfortable. Another is that these approaches may not have been very effective in the past. We freely acknowledge that there is room for honest debate about which practices are likely to be most effective, but it is important not to allow disagreements to prompt an anything-goes policy.

A second choice is to set a rigorous standard for determining whether an approach is acceptable. The National Reading Panel (National Institute of Child Health and Human Development, 2000) used this standard in examining the research base underlying a range of instructional approaches. They insisted that judgments about an approach be based on closely controlled experimental and quasi-experimental investigations. Studies of this kind are said to be "scientific" because they are designed to determine whether particular approaches are more effective than others. This is the method of research used in medicine, such as when a new drug is compared with another drug or a placebo.

Setting so high a standard has obvious appeal, but there are also pitfalls. For example, some promising approaches may as yet have few experimental studies to validate their effectiveness. Moreover, even where such studies have been conducted, the results may not generalize to populations and grade levels not examined in the studies. Finally, Goeke and Ritchey (2008) warn that insistence on scientifically based practices can cause unnecessary divisiveness among teachers. They warn that arguments about which instructional practices to implement at each tier can threaten the sense of community within a school. Limiting acceptable approaches to those with a scientific pedigree is sure to exacerbate tensions.

Nevertheless, decisions must be made about which practices to endorse, which to discourage, and which to target through professional development. Consequently, we recommend a third choice. It involves casting a broader net in identifying effective instructional approaches. In essence, it represents the middle ground between scientific rigor and anything goes. This choice results in a viable list of effective approaches, one that permits options but also constrains them in important ways.

Sources of Approaches and Interventions

Let's begin with an important distinction. By *approach*, we mean a method of instruction that can be employed outside a commercial system. An *intervention*, on the other hand, is more comprehensive and formal. It often contains its own assessments and may embody a number of approaches. Because a comprehensive RTI system requires both strategies and interventions, information on each is essential. The search strategies, however, are considerably different.

To get an idea of whether an approach is likely to work, we need information about the research conducted to confirm its effectiveness. However, we are not suggesting that you conduct a comprehensive literature review. A more practical strategy is to rely on secondary sources that report the results of such reviews. You might begin with the approaches identified by the National Reading Panel (National Institute of Child Health and Human Development, 2000) and add to them judiciously based on subsequent reviews. Recently, federal agencies have produced several short teacher-friendly research reviews that are a good starting point for learning about the converging research evidence in a few key areas (e.g., Armbruster, Lehr, & Osborn, 2001; Gersten et al., 2008; Lehr, Osborn, & Hiebert, 2004; Shanahan et al., 2010) Practitioner-oriented books can be helpful as tools for distilling the lessons of research—provided the authors subscribe to the belief that comparative studies can inform the question of effectiveness. For example, Walpole and McKenna (2007, 2009) settled on six approaches to vocabulary instruction based on available findings. These were concept of definition, semantic feature analysis, concept sorting, semantic maps, graphic organizers, and text talk. This is only an example, of course. Other sources may well offer different lists. We suspect, though, that there will be more commonality than differences because all authors are using the same research base. Remember too that extensive lists are unnecessary, and they may even work against the efforts of coaching and other forms of professional development. Compiling a few effective strategies in each area of reading instruction will meet most needs.

Information on interventions requires a different strategy. Commercial programs are typically not the subject of peer-reviewed studies (there are notable exceptions), but sources of evidence nevertheless exist. This evidence might take the form of comparison studies and it might also amount to an inspection of the instructional approaches embraced within the intervention. Reviews of interventions sometimes appear in book form (e.g., O'Connor & Vadasy, 2011). Additional sources include the National Center on Response to Intervention (*www.rti4success. org*), the What Works Clearinghouse (*http://ies.ed.gov/ncee/wwc*), and the Best Evidence Encyclopedia (*www.bestevidence.org*).

PROFESSIONAL DEVELOPMENT IN THE RTI SYSTEM

The word *creating* in the title of this chapter does not mean merely developing an RTI system on paper but implementing it in practice. Full implementation requires that every professional understand how the RTI system is supposed to function, how assessments are used to inform instructional decisions, and which approaches to instruction are deemed most effective.

The role of professional development in bringing about these understandings is enormous. For those who find the sheer scope a little daunting, we offer this bit of guidance: *Make assessment central.* In an RTI system, assessments help to identify instructional needs, they help in selecting approaches and programs, and they help gauge their effectiveness. Ultimately, they help inform decisions about movement across tiers. Grasping how assessments work to accomplish these aims is really to grasp the RTI system itself.

Ensuring Teacher Understanding through Professional Development

The knowledge teachers need to function effectively in an RTI system is broad and multidimensional. They must understand the logic underlying tiered instruction and the reasons RTI is supplanting the older IQ-deficit model. They must be aware not only of the types of assessments and their roles in an RTI system, but also of the specific assessments they are expected to use, when to administer them, and how to interpret them. Finally, they must be cognizant of instructional approaches that are most likely to have a positive influence on achievement. They must also be *willing* and *able* to implement those techniques. These are two very different qualities. For some teachers the instructional approaches embraced in RTI may be at odds with prior experience and philosophy. To sum up, teachers must understand the rationale behind RTI. The assessments required must become almost second nature, a part of standard operating procedure. And they must apply specific research-based techniques when assessments indicate the need for it.

The goals of professional development, when stated in this manner, may seem daunting. They should. RTI requires major changes in the way schools go about the business of education, changes that involve nearly every professional on the faculty. Professional development is essential if these individuals are to implement RTI in a way that works. It involves not only teachers but specialists and administrators, who suddenly find their responsibilities redefined by the new system.

There are two approaches to implementation and each dictates a different approach to professional development. One approach is to hit the ground running and do it all at once. Teacher knowledge must be built quickly and applied almost immediately as they learn *and* administer new assessments, learn *and* use new instructional approaches, learn *and* apply new methods of grouping, and learn *and* enact new ways of collaborating with specialists. So much so soon can create tremendous pressures on classroom teachers, administrators, and specialists. It can lead to frustration and even confusion. Research on school change argues against rapidly imposed schoolwide initiatives. On the other hand, the achievement crisis in many schools is sometimes characterized as an emergency.

The second approach is slower and more methodical. It phases in RTI, beginning with extensive professional development and the careful selection of assessments and materials that will be used. Some professional development is provided prior to implementation of the full system, and it is designed to build teacher understanding in a systematic way. There is time to build knowledge collaboratively, through discussion of common sources in teacher study groups. Such groups "allow teachers to focus on individual goals while interacting on a larger scale with professional colleagues" (Bean & Morewood, 2011, p. 468). After implementation begins, professional development continues, but it transitions from general knowledge building to real applications with children and classrooms. Once the RTI system is launched, teachers will continue to require support as they use assessments to plan instruction and to evaluate the effects of that instruction. What they have learned in the abstract must be applied in real settings.

Whether the pace of implementation is fast or slow, key individuals must take on the responsibility for guiding it. We deliberately use the plural because an initiative as broad as RTI cannot be managed by a single person. It must be a team effort and leadership from a number of individuals will be needed if implementation is to succeed.

Metropolitan Elementary Launches Its 2-Year Plan

Metropolitan Elementary developed a 2-year implementation plan for RTI. The district did not mandate a particular plan or schedule, but the district leaders did approve Metropolitan Elementary's plan before it was launched. In brief, the first year would be devoted to building teacher knowledge, deciding on assessments and materials, and working on the mechanics of how the plan would work. On paper, the working draft of the plan was deliberately vague. Those who drafted it included the school principal, Ms. Hamilton (the literacy coach), and the school's lead special education teachers. They were cautious about being overly specific because they knew that many formative changes would need to be made once the actual implementation began during the second year. Their suspicion that unanticipated developments would arise proved all too accurate. Each year brought about changes that were difficult to predict and that required flexible responses in order to keep the initiative on track.

Year 1 focused primarily on four aims: (1) establishing an RTI design team that would guide the implementation, (2) providing the professional development needed to create a mutual understanding of RTI in general and how the Metropolitan Elementary plan in particular would work, (3) ensuring that appropriate Tier 1 assessments were in place, and (4) choosing and purchasing materials for intensive intervention. The RTI design team included the principal as an ex officio member but was chaired by Ms. Hamilton. The team also included one of the school's three special education teachers as well as the grade-level chair for each grade (K–5). A team of nine may seem somewhat unwieldy, but the principal thought that a broad representation was important for an initiative as comprehensive as RTI. It was especially wise that each grade be represented because of differences in the assessments that would be needed. Additionally, the school psychologist and EL teacher were often included in the meetings.

Team members read a common set of materials chosen by Ms. Hamilton and the special education leader. These materials were wide ranging in nature. They included books, articles, chapters, and Internet resources such as podcasts and videos. The materials represented different perspectives and addressed both the standard and problem-solving protocols. Although the decision to implement the standard protocol in Tier 2 had already been made, the diagnostic strategies entailed in the problem-solving approach would still be applied in Tier 3 and were therefore included in the readings. For the entire fall semester, the RTI design team met weekly as a study group, facilitated by Ms. Hamilton. Toward the end of the fall term, the team made decisions about which of the materials they wished teachers to read. The result was in effect an RTI professional development curriculum. The team chose the materials, arranged them in a logical order, and established a spring schedule for grade-level meetings. Together with a few guiding questions suggested by Ms. Hamilton, the materials included a combination of print and digital resources. The latter were uploaded to the district's Moodle[1] site. Major topics were studied in this order:

1. Introduction to RTI and the two principal approaches
2. Assessments needed to drive an RTI system
3. How to conduct an assessment audit (including an actual audit)
4. Basics of data interpretation
5. Role of the reading specialist and special education teachers
6. Research-based approaches to differentiated instruction

The grade-level study groups were facilitated by either Ms. Hamilton or one of the special education teachers. Her choices of which topics she would take on entailed an honest appraisal of her own expertise. For example, she knew that her knowledge of data interpretation was limited, so she asked a special education teacher to take the lead on that topic. Zigmond and Kloo (2012) point out that this area is typically a strength of special educators and represents an important contribution they

---

[1] Moodle is one of several available systems for housing digital resources, facilitating dialogue, and so on. We chose it arbitrarily for this example.

can make to professional development related to RTI. Discussions during group meetings were engaging for the most part, and teachers felt free to express their responses to the content of the materials.

Prior to the start of the school year, the team met with educators at different schools in the district to learn about DIBELS Next, which had been selected by the district as a universal screening system.[2] Use of the same screening system across schools is the best way to track students and to build mutual understandings among teachers. The fall term began with the administration of the DIBELS Next battery. The main purpose of the testing was to establish baseline data at each grade level in order to get a clear picture of where Metropolitan Elementary stood as a school. In other words, the measures were not used as the first step in the screening–diagnostic one-two punch we have described in this book. A SWAT team approach was used during the first year, consisting of Ms. Hamilton, Ms. Chern (the reading specialist), and the three special education teachers, to disrupt instruction as little as possible.

The first year ended with a widespread understanding of RTI on the part of Metropolitan Elementary's teachers and a professional development curriculum that could be adapted to mentor new hires. An end-of-year administration of DIBELS Next provided a means of gauging the progress made by children at each grade level in several key dimensions of reading. The intent of this pre–post testing was to paint an accurate portrait of reading growth under the status quo. The results were not pretty, nor were they unexpected. After all, Metropolitan Elementary's teachers serve a challenging population and the school had fallen short of its AYP goals for several years. The DIBELS Next results confirmed that there was work to be done and illuminated areas where change might be most beneficial.

The first year had its share of unanticipated consequences. The special education teachers had been happy enough with the IQ-deficit model they had used in the past, and one was skeptical about the idea of pushing in to regular education classrooms to work with children without IEPs. This was one of the more contentious ideas the team had read about. One other unexpected development arose. To the surprise of the principal, some of the teachers were unhappy with the slow pace of change. After all, an entire year had been spent on preparation while no student had actually received the benefits of RTI. Teachers were unsure about whether they could still refer children for special education evaluation or whether the children had to go through tiers of instruction. This would change during the second year.

Coaching after Implementation

Because RTI has so many moving parts, there are many places where the system might break down. And because even the best-intentioned teachers will face

---

[2] Again, we choose DIBELS Next arbitrarily for this example.

uncharacteristic challenges, they will require support if they are to make real contributions to the system. Coaching has the potential to provide support and help the moving parts work together more smoothly.

A school fortunate enough to have an experienced literacy coach, one who understands the school context and has developed relationships with specific teachers, is in a position to implement RTI more quickly and effectively than other schools. Schools without a coach can nevertheless require one or more individuals to assume a "coachlike" role as implementation gets underway. In the case of Metropolitan Elementary, that individual was Ms. Hamilton. Her extensive experience as a reading specialist gave her a foundation on which to provide coaching assistance. But effective coaching requires other qualities as well. Coaching requires an understanding of adult learning and how it requires instructional approaches that differ from those used with children (McKenna & Walpole, 2008). It requires the ability to gather and interpret data that document achievement and are useful in planning instruction. It requires the capacity to forge productive relationships with colleagues, including those who resist a particular initiative. It also requires the humility necessary to learn from those coached, the willingness to lend whatever assistance they may need to succeed, and the habits of reflecting on events in order to distill their lessons.

This is a tall order, to be sure, and few of the coaches we have encountered have possessed all of these characteristics. It is hardly surprising that reading specialists, whose responsibilities have largely involved working with small numbers of challenged children prior to RTI, are frequently perplexed by the new set of proficiencies needed for implementation. We believe that an advantage of RTI lies in the specificity of the plan. That is to say, when all involved understand exactly what is required by the system, coaching becomes a means of moving individuals in the direction of a common goal, one that has been made explicit through the RTI plan. The advantage lies in the fact that expectations are nonnegotiable. In some models of coaching, this is not the case and a coach's focus may be limited to matters that are only remotely connected to instructional effectiveness.

McKenna and Walpole (2008) have compared coaching to the hardness scale used to classify rocks. At the "softer" end, coaching involves acceptance of teachers' professional judgments about the sort of professional development they need. A coach's efforts usually entail fine tuning of a teacher's current practice or learning new approaches that are minimal disruptions to established ways of doing things. In contrast, "harder" models of coaching begin with a clear idea of the instructional approaches that should be in place. Coaching involves taking stock of existing practice and then nudging teachers in the direction of the desired set of approaches. We believe that reform-oriented coaching (the harder variety) is required for successful implementation. This means that a coach cannot afford to ignore resistant teachers and hope they will come around later on, as some have suggested (e.g., Hoffman & Sailors, 2008). It also means that the principal must show complete support for the coach's efforts and that multiple avenues must be pursued in developing teacher knowledge and, when necessary, altering their belief structures.

In the case of phased implementation, knowledge-building sessions such as book studies might give way to data interpretation, group formation, targeted observations, and follow-up conferences. Although these approaches to professional development are common in "softer" models of coaching, they take on an edge in the reform-oriented coaching needed in RTI precisely because of the clear vision of where teachers need to be. Coaching needs to occur concurrently with implementation activities, such as gathering and analyzing data. And in fact these activities provide a specific focus for coaching, making it more objective and less personal in nature. The transition of coaching from knowledge building to reshaping instructional practice is evident in our example of Metropolitan Elementary as the school moves into its second year of RTI.

Metropolitan Elementary Moves into Year 2

Year 2 began once again with DIBELS Next testing. This time, however, Ms. Hamilton presented a summary of the results for each grade level during a "state-of-the-school" talk at the opening faculty meeting (Walpole & McKenna, 2012). Results were not broken down by classroom because doing so might have embarrassed individual teachers. However, classroom profiles were presented at grade-level meetings and on a one-to-one basis by Ms. Hamilton. Working with individual teachers, Ms. Hamilton pointed the way to the next assessments. The expectation was that the classroom teachers would administer them and that small groups will be formed in collaboration with Ms. Hamilton. When she revisited the teachers 2 weeks later to help them form small groups, she discovered that several of the teachers had not administered the follow-up assessments, complaining that they had not been able to find the time. Thereafter, Ms. Hamilton made an effort to give these assessments herself.

To her relief, she soon discovered that most of the children in each classroom were rather easily grouped for Tier 1 differentiated instruction but that a few did not seem to fit into any of the small-group configurations. Working in collaboration with the teachers at each grade level, she worked out compromise placements for some children. At first grade, for example, where the teachers had strong collaborative relationships, she crafted a system in which a handful of children moved across classroom boundaries for small-group instruction. This plan worked well for addressing the needs of children who were too few in number to be grouped efficiently within any one classroom, and it avoided the problems associated with regrouping for the entire literacy block.

Ms. Hamilton created an Excel spreadsheet that included all of the children in school. It documented DIBELS Next scores as well as information about small-group placement. She also reserved columns for entering notes about what approaches were tried and for how long. In short, she began a tracking system that was efficient and not overly labor intensive. Every 3 weeks, she requested that each teacher present progress monitoring results for those students performing below benchmark. She entered the results into her spreadsheet and also wrote the name of every child at Metropolitan Elementary on color-coded stickies attached to a data wall in her office. The data wall served as a visible reminder of where the children were and provided a convenient reference when she met with teachers.

Overall, Ms. Hamilton worked hard to set up a tracking system that was sensitive to growth and useful in making the hard decisions about Tier 2 and Tier 3 instruction. It looked great in Excel. But problems arose in getting it to work. Many teachers, especially the younger ones, were enthusiastic about the RTI system and appreciated the structure and guidance it provided. Some teachers, on the other hand, exhibited what amounted to passive–aggressive behavior. They agreed to the groupings but provided instruction that was very different from what was expected. As a result, their students registered only modest gains on progress monitoring measures, creating a coaching problem that was awkward to address. A few teachers were openly resistant to targeting deficits through instruction that was, even temporarily, outside the context of meaningful encounters with print in the form of leveled books. Ms. Hamilton decided to challenge such teachers through some informal, action research. She persuaded one first-grade teacher to help her conduct a modest study with a group of 12 students who displayed similar decoding deficits. All were first given the Informal Phonics Inventory (McKenna & Stahl, 2009) at the beginning of a 6-week interval. These students were then assigned to Ms. Hamilton's group or the teacher's group based on the results of the phonics inventory and the Elementary Spelling Inventory. Ms. Hamilton used the inventory results to plan targeted instruction and administered a DIBELS Next NWF progress monitoring test to all 12 students every 3 to 4 weeks. Of the six students in Ms. Hamilton's group, four now exceeded the benchmark and the other two were within a stone's throw within 6 weeks. Only one of the classroom teacher's six students showed comparable gains. In discussing the results, Ms. Hamilton was careful to make three points. First, these were the very children already assigned to the teacher, who could not argue that "this would never work with my kids." Second, Ms. Hamilton pointed out that she had done nothing special with her group. She had simply applied the instructional approaches that have been presented during professional development. Finally, she stressed the fact that running records indicated that the six children in her skills-based group had also made more progress in reading increasingly difficult levels of text than children in the other group.

Ms. Hamilton's experience with this classroom study convinced her that teachers must perceive that change is in the best interest of their children if they are to accept it. She had considered citing a study she had encountered that produced similar results with first graders (Walpole, McKenna, Coker, & Philippakos, 2010), but doing so probably would not have succeeded in changing the teacher's practice.

Playing the "research card" is rarely effective. On the other hand, action studies engage teachers in inquiry they find important. "Teachers formulate questions for which they want answers," Bean and Morewood observe. "Teacher research also increases the opportunity for teachers to become decision makers, problem solvers, and school leaders. It gives teachers opportunities to interact with an idea or data that promotes reflection and thinking" (2011, p. 469).

Year 2 also saw the implementation at Tiers 2 and 3 under the RTI system. These dimensions of RTI could not wait for Year 3 because the assessment system was soon tracking some students through differentiated instruction that was not proving to be effective. The school adopted two commercial programs for use in Tier 2 instruction. One program focused on phonological awareness, phonics, and fluency. The other commercial program emphasized reading comprehension development. Both programs had high ratings for effectiveness in the What Works Clearinghouse and Best Evidence Encyclopedia. The more intensive instruction at the higher tiers was somewhat easier to manage because fewer teachers were involved and all had had extensive preparation in meeting the needs of challenging youngsters. Additionally, Ms. Hamilton and the lead special education teacher were very involved in their respective professional organizations. They attended local and national conferences in order to stay up-to-date on the latest research-based practice and they each subscribed to professional journals.

Ms. Hamilton created an additional tab on her Excel spreadsheet for tracking these children, and the information she compiled proved indispensable in making referrals for those children who were unresponsive to the intensive instruction they received at higher tiers.

Several challenges arose involving these tiers, however. One concerned scheduling. Ms. Hamilton and the three special education teachers leapfrogged from room to room and grade to grade through most of the morning, pushing in to teach small groups. Their schedules in the afternoon were also crammed with preexisting commitments. For example, the special education teachers needed to serve students who were already classified and had IEPs. When openings in the schedule did present themselves, they often required pulling children out of their classrooms at inconvenient times. Because so many educators were affected by the scheduling issues, the principal had to take an active role in crafting a workable solution.

Another challenge involved the commercial materials that had been purchased for use at Tier 2. The teachers discovered that these were not panaceas and that they had uneven effects on children's learning. Two of the special education teachers investigated alternative programs, which had garnered positive reviews and the endorsement of their colleagues at other schools. Because relatively few children were to be taught with these programs, the principal was able to find the funds necessary to purchase a few kits. Ms. Hamilton and the special education teachers met several times to discuss all the materials used in Tier 2, and they made notes concerning what kinds of students tended to be responsive to each.

Ms. Hamilton did not make the mistake of neglecting professional development during Year 2. However, she transitioned from leading study groups to facilitating teachers' understanding of data trends. She met with teachers in grade groups every 3 weeks to review the movement of struggling readers toward benchmark status. In reviewing class profiles and tracking individual students, Ms. Hamilton and the classroom teachers learned together. She soon discovered that many of her veteran teachers had useful insights to share now that RTI had provided a framework for focusing the reflection.

As a coach, Ms. Hamilton viewed the need for professional development as all inclusive. She recognized that classroom teachers were not the only educators at Metropolitan Elementary who could benefit from professional development. Ms. Hamilton herself, Ms. Chern, and the special education teachers were filling new roles because of RTI, and she knew they would need to grow in order to adapt. Coaching specialists, however, presented sensitive issues. She knew she must honor their prior knowledge and skills but at the same time get them to acknowledge a need for professional learning. She approached this task by forming a separate study group. The main focus was on instructional strategies appropriate at Tier 3. All five members of this group had much to learn in this area. In the past, the special education teachers had relied primarily on kits, such as those used at Tier 2, and Ms. Chern had typically applied approaches that amounted for the most part to adaptations of Tier 1 methods. Leadership of the group was shared. Each member was responsible for identifying research-based strategies and presenting them to the group on a rotating basis. Ms. Hamilton organized resource notebooks containing articles that described the approaches. She also created a chart that mapped each approach the group studied to the deficit it was designed to address. She expanded this chart throughout the year, and it served as the first page of each member's notebook.

EVALUATING AN RTI SYSTEM

Albers and colleagues (2005) make an important distinction between assessment *for* intervention and assessment *of* intervention. At first blush, this may seem to be a distinction without a difference. That is, if we want to know how well the RTI system is working, we need only look at changes in student achievement. It is certainly true that student outcomes are the bottom line. However, outcome measures can tell us little or nothing about the strengths and weaknesses of RTI in a school. When student growth is less than we had hoped for, we need to be able to identify problem areas so that we can address them. In a sense, evaluating RTI should follow the same logic we use to evaluate a child. We begin with a broad screening measure (in this case, our bottom-line indicators of student achievement) and we move next to "diagnostic" measures designed to pinpoint areas that require attention.

The goal of evaluation must be to create a formative cycle through which weak student growth triggers a systematic examination of the components of RTI, followed by attempts to address trouble spots. As Hoffman and Sailors put it, "Good evaluation supports a cycle of growth" (2008, p. 250). We have depicted this cycle in Figure 8.1.

Examining the components of an RTI system requires looking systematically at data of various kinds, including:

- Screening results for each area
  - Expressed in terms of movement across risk levels
  - Broken down by grade level and teacher
- Teacher concerns that are systemic in nature
- Observational data to gauge the degree of implementation

Information of different types from a variety of sources helps to confirm where trouble may lie.

Taking Stock of RTI at Metropolitan Elementary

At Metropolitan Elementary, it was not until the end of Year 2 that a reasonable appraisal of the RTI framework was possible. During postplanning days, Ms. Hamilton presented the results of the DIBELS Next assessments in her second state-of-the-school address. Although DIBELS Next and AIMSweb are used chiefly as screening and progress monitoring tools, they can also shed light on the progress made collectively at each grade level. Of special importance is the percentage of children who move from one risk level to another. This percentage is more telling than simple changes in mean scores. It is almost inevitable for mean increases to be observed, but the true significance lies in the reduction of risk. Risk thresholds

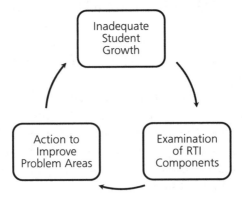

FIGURE 8.1. Formative cycle of evaluation of the RTI system.

have been determined through predictive studies, and reducing the level of risk is associated with a higher level of success during the following year. Ms. Hamilton created several PowerPoint slides to illustrate how students moved across risk levels. As before, she did not single out individual teachers, though she planned to share classroom growth charts individually. For presentation to the whole faculty, she focused on grade-level results. Figure 8.2 presents one of the slides she created. It illustrates a before-and-after comparison of first-grade students at each risk level on the NWF subtest. Ms. Hamilton was careful to include only those students who had both fall and spring scores because the idea was to gauge the impact of instruction at Metropolitan Elementary overall. Students who arrived or left during the course of the year might have skewed the results and given an inaccurate picture of RTI's impact. Interpreting the results involved a classic glass-half-full–glass-half-empty choice. Clearly, the percentage of students at high risk diminished, but a significant percentage remained. This particular comparison had to be considered together with the results of the other DIBELS Next subtests at each grade level and also with additional measurements. Ms. Hamilton did her best to draw reasonable conclusions about the reading program at Metropolitan Elementary, and she consulted with her colleagues on the RTI leadership team before summarizing them for the entire faculty.

Ms. Hamilton was cautious about attributing student growth to RTI. To be sure, Year 1 results had provided a baseline against which to compare the growth made during Year 2. She prepared additional slides, like the one in Figure 8.3, to enable such comparisons. Her goal was to contrast the trend for first-grade NWF

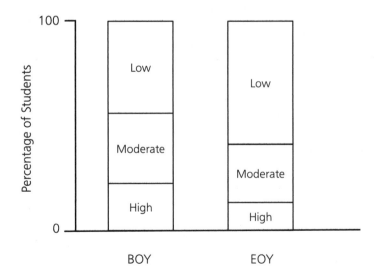

FIGURE 8.2. Graph used to illustrate movement across risk levels. BOY, beginning of year; EOY, end of year.

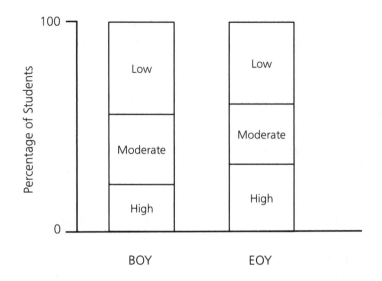

FIGURE 8.3. Graph depicting risk levels before RTI. BOY, beginning of year; EOY, end of year.

during the baseline year (Year 1) with the trend during the first year of implementation (Year 2), depicted in Figure 8.2. The results are indeed striking. However, she also decided to follow the advice of Hoffman and Sailors (2008) and consult a measurement specialist. The head of assessment at the district office was encouraging but warned her that these were different cohorts of children, that the faculty had changed slightly at Metropolitan Elementary, and that schools are complex places in general, where many factors influence achievement. These considerations qualified her comparison of Years 1 and 2 and she candidly shared these cautions. Nevertheless, the changes were largely positive and she felt comfortable in lauding the teachers for their efforts.

The year-end appraisal had its rough spots as well. For example, percentages of third-grade children at high risk on the ORF subtest did not change appreciably between Years 1 and 2. These instances underscore the importance of gathering qualitative information, such as anecdotal notations made throughout the year, to help explain where the process may be breaking down. In the case of third grade, Ms. Hamilton noted that the overall pattern was largely attributable to two of the five third-grade teachers, who did not implement small-group instruction based on the assessed needs of their students. She hoped that the classroom-level results would arm her with the evidence she needed to alter the beliefs of these two teachers when they were able to contrast their records with those of their three colleagues.

Ms. Hamilton did not rely on DIBELS Next alone to base pre–post comparisons. She recognized that a fair number of teachers were skeptical of the subskill orientation of DIBELS Next, and so she also kept records of the guided reading levels of students. She was able to present profiles at each grade level that opened an additional window on student achievement. Figure 8.4 represents the second-grade distribution of children by guided reading level at the beginning and end of Year 2. Because these levels are not easily quantified, she did not attempt to "average" the levels. However, the two bar graphs provided ample grist for discussion. Clearly, the two distributions documented movement to the right over the course of the year, toward more challenging texts, but the percentage of children below the end-of-year benchmark level (Fountas & Pinnell, 2006, Level N) was far too high. Ms. Hamilton made a point of showing how the results of DIBELS Next were largely congruent with the progress documented through guided reading levels, and she underscored the fact that the fine-grained nature of the DIBELS Next subtests provided the specific guidance required for administering the diagnostics necessary to differentiate instruction.

Ms. Hamilton did rely on her analysis of test scores alone to evaluate the RTI program at Metropolitan Elementary. They did reveal problem areas, to be sure, but an understanding of these problems came through other sorts of information. For example, the two third-grade teachers whose students had showed little gain had long been on her radar. She had conducted observations during small-group time and discovered that their implementation of effective approaches was problematic. These teachers represented instances where quantitative indicators (DIBELS Next scores) led to qualitative follow-up (observation). Some problems, however, do not manifest themselves directly in achievement results. Several first-grade teachers,

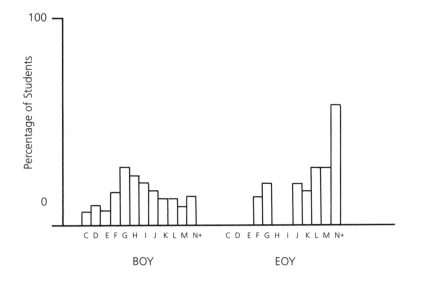

FIGURE 8.4. Beginning- and end-of-year distributions of guided reading levels at grade 2. BOY, beginning of year; EOY, end of year.

for instance, had come to her with scheduling conflicts that might have limited the amount of small-group time available. Early attention to such matters is also part of the evaluation of an RTI system.

Addressing Trouble Spots

Sources of trouble can be divided into two general categories: logistical and personal. Logistical problems include matters of scheduling, test administration and scoring, interpretation of data, formation of groups, appraising the effectiveness of commercial programs, and tracking students across time and tiers. Personal problems involve individual teachers who, for one reason or another, are not functioning well within the RTI plan. They may be resistant to the instruction required by RTI. They may be unaccustomed to collaborating with their peers. They may fail to engage in study group activities. They may simply feel uncomfortable with their new roles. Coaching can help to alleviate these problems, but there are many demands on a coach's time. Personal situations must be prioritized so that those likely to have the greatest impact on student learning receive the earliest attention.

Keeping the End in Mind

This advice (freely adapted from Steven Covey) is an instinctively good notion but is short on specifics. Exactly what "end" should be kept in mind? Making the ultimate goal of RTI implementation as specific as possible is an important component of evaluation. An approach we recommend is called an innovation configuration (Hall & Hord, 2006; Hord, 1986). We begin by listing the key components of the RTI framework. We next describe what a strong implementation of each component should look like. We then describe the beginning and intermediate stages of implementation. The result is a matrix in which one row is devoted to each component.

We created the innovation configuration matrix in Table 8.1 to help capture the big picture of implementation. Determining ratings for each component will require using an assortment of data. This process is admittedly subjective, but it can provide an aerial view of implementation and lead to a more specific examination of troublesome areas. It affords a tool for occasional reflection about the big picture of RTI, a tool that helps us keep the end in mind.

TABLE 8.1. Innovation Configuration for RTI Implementation

RTI component	Level of implementation		
	Weak	In progress	Strong
Screening assessments	Screening is done incorrectly or incompletely	Complete data are collected at three benchmark points, but results are often not used appropriately	Screening data are frequently used to determine the need for diagnostics and to form small groups
Diagnostics	Diagnostic assessments are not consistently given and/or used to plan instruction	Diagnostic assessments are used by a significant percentage of teachers	Diagnostic assessments are used by nearly all teachers as a follow-up to screening
Progress monitoring	Progress monitoring of students at risk is done rarely or inconsistently	Progress monitoring of students at risk is done for most students at risk	Progress monitoring of students at risk is done for nearly all students at risk
Tier 1 differentiation	Teachers often form inappropriate groups and/or use inappropriate instructional methods	Most teachers group on the basis of assessments and provide appropriate instruction	Nearly all teachers group on the basis of assessments and provide appropriate instruction
Tier 2	Appropriate Tier 2 instruction is rarely provided when data indicate a need for it	Appropriate Tier 2 instruction is provided for some of the students who need it	Appropriate Tier 2 instruction is provided for nearly all of the students who need it
Tier 3	Tier 3 instruction is rarely provided when data indicate a need for it	Appropriate Tier 3 instruction is provided for some of the students who need it	Appropriate Tier 3 instruction is provided for nearly all of the students who need it
Special education referral system	Referrals are rarely based on data indicating lack of responsiveness to Tier 3 intervention	Referrals are often based on data indicating lack of responsiveness to Tier 3 intervention	Referrals are always based on data indicating lack of responsiveness to Tier 3 intervention
Data system	No comprehensive system is in place for storing data for students and groups over time	A comprehensive system is in place for storing data, but information is incomplete or hard to access and summarize	A comprehensive system is in place for storing data and it is routinely used to track student progress efficiently and make appropriate decisions
Professional development	Professional development has been limited or has resulted in inadequate knowledge of RTI and how to achieve its expectations	Professional development has led to adequate knowledge of RTI and its expectations for a large proportion of teachers	Professional development has led to adequate knowledge of RTI and its expectations for nearly all teachers and has entered a fine-tuning stage for most

Internet Resources That Support RTI Implementation

CBM ASSESSMENTS AND DATA MANAGEMENT

AIMSweb (available for purchase)
www.aimsweb.com
Skills: Early reading, oral reading, comprehension, spelling, writing, math
Tests: Screening, Progress Monitoring

- Early reading measures are available in Spanish
- Cross-year data management

DIBELS (available free)
https://dibels.uoregon.edu
Skills: Early reading, oral reading, comprehension
Tests: Screening, Progress Monitoring

- Available in Spanish
- Cross-year data management

CBM GENERATOR AND GRAPHING TOOLS

Intervention Central (available free)
www.interventioncentral.org

- Graph maker
- Letter name fluency generator
- Word list fluency generator (based on Dolch words)
- Reading fluency passage generator

- Maze passage generator
- Writing probe generator

INTERVENTION REVIEWS

Educators may find it difficult to access, read, and evaluate all of the research on particular interventions and commercial products. Panels of researchers review the research and critically analyze research evidence that is reported on these websites. Concise summaries of the strengths and weaknesses of each commercial reading or intervention program are posted in consumer report formats. This allows schools to have confidence in their selection of evidence-based interventions.

Best Evidence Encyclopedia
www.bestevidence.org

What Works Clearinghouse
http://ies.ed.gov/ncee/wwc

RESOURCES FROM NATIONAL RESEARCH CENTERS AND PROFESSIONAL ORGANIZATIONS

These sites contain a range of resources including RTI webinars, how-to guides, overviews of assessments, and overviews of interventions.

International Reading Association
www.reading.org/Resources/ResourcesByTopic/ResponseToIntervention/Overview.aspx

National Center on Response to Intervention
www.rti4success.org

- Comparison of screening tools:
  www.rti4success.org/screeningtools
  Comparison of progress monitoring tools: *www.rti4success.org/progressmonitoringtools*
- Comparison of intervention programs
  www.rti4success.org/instructiontools

National Research Center on Learning Disabilities
www.nrcld.org

- How to do it guide with check sheets:
  www.nrcld.org/rti_manual

RTI Action Network
www.rtinetwork.org

STATE RTI RESOURCES

NYS RTI Technical Assistance Center
www.nysrti.org

Resources collected by New York's RTI Technical Assistance Center including professional development modules, articles, webinars, parent resources, and the state's guidance document for implementing RTI are available to the public on this website.

- Pilot schools:
  www.nysrti.org/page/pilot-schools

This site provides detailed information about the ongoing RTI implementation process undertaken by 14 schools throughout the state of New York. Each school posts its year-by-year action plan, assessment audit, a description of tiered interventions, and the decision tree for movement between tiers. This provides a nice portrait of how different schools with a range of demographics and resources continue to refine their RTI model. No two models are alike, but all include the principal components of RTI.
For information on accessing other individual state resources:
http://state.rti4success.org/index.php

UNIVERSITY RESOURCES

These websites contain a range of resources that can be used to support schools in applying research-based practice in classroom and intervention settings. These sites provide assessment, instructional, and professional development materials. Tools such as principal walk-through sheets, professional development modules, instructional materials, and case studies may be accessed on these websites. Because the university is the heart of research, the most up-to-date research reports may be found on these sites.

Florida Center for Reading Research
www.fcrr.org

Iris Center at Vanderbilt
http://iris.peabody.vanderbilt.edu

References

Albers, C. A., Elliott, S. N., Kettler, R. J., & Roach, A. T. (2005). Evaluating intervention outcomes. In R. Brown-Chidsey (Ed.), *Assessment for intervention: A problem-solving approach* (pp. 329–351). New York: Guilford Press.

Allington, R. L. (1983). Fluency: The neglected reading goal. *The Reading Teacher, 37,* 556–561.

Armbruster, B. B., Lehr, F., & Osborn, J. (2001). *Put reading first: The research building blocks for teaching children to read.* Washington, DC: Partnership for Reading. Retrieved from *www.nifl.gov.*

Bean, R. M., & Morewood, A. L. (2011). Best practices in professional development for improving literacy instruction in schools. In L. M. Morrow & L. B. Gambrell (Eds.), *Best practices in literacy instruction* (4th ed., pp. 455–478). New York: Guilford Press.

Bear, D. R., Invernizzi, M., Templeton, S., & Johnston, F. (2011). *Words their way: Word study for phonics, vocabulary, and spelling instruction* (5th ed.). Upper Saddle River, NJ: Pearson Education.

Beaver, J. (1997). *Developmental reading assessment.* Glenview, IL: Celebration Press.

Beck I. L., McKeown, M. G., & Kucan, L. (2002). *Bringing words to life: Robust vocabulary instruction.* New York: Guilford Press.

Benjamin, R. G., & Schwanenflugel, P. J. (2010). Text complexity and oral reading prosody in young readers. *Reading Research Quarterly, 45*(4), 388–404.

Biemiller, A. (2012). Teaching vocabulary in the primary grades: Vocabulary instruction needed. In E. J. Kameenui & J. F. Baumann (Eds.), *Vocabulary instruction: Research to practice* (2nd ed., pp. 34–50). New York: Guilford Press.

Blachowicz, C., & Fisher, P. J. (2009). *Teaching vocabulary in all classrooms* (4th ed.). Upper Saddle River, NJ: Pearson Education.

Brown-Chidsey, R. (2005). The role of published norm-referenced tests in problem-solving-based assessment. In R. Brown-Chidsey (Ed.), *Assessment for intervention: A problem-solving approach* (pp. 247–264). New York: Guilford Press.

Brown-Chidsey, R., & Steege, M. W. (2005). *Response to intervention: Principles and strategies for effective practice.* New York: Guilford Press.

Burns, M. K., Christ, T. J., Boice, C. H., & Szadokierski, I. (2010). Special education in an RTI model: Addressing unique learning needs. In T. A. Glover & S. Vaughn (Eds.), *The promise of response to intervention: Evaluating current science and practice* (pp. 267–285). New York: Guilford Press.

Clay, M. M. (2005). *Literacy lessons: Designed for individuals, part two.* Portsmouth, NH: Heinemann.

Clay, M. M. (2006). *An observation survey of early literacy achievement.* Portsmouth, NH: Heinemann.

Common Core State Standards Initiative. (2010). *Common Core State Standards for English Language Arts & Literacy in History/Social Studies, Science, and Technical Subjects.* Washington, DC: National Governors Association Center for Best Practices and the Council of Chief State School Officers.

Connor, C. M., Morrison, F. J., & Katch, L. E. (2004). Beyond the reading wars: Exploring the effect of child–instruction interactions in growth in early reading. *Scientific Studies of Reading, 8,* 305–336.

Cummings, K. D., Kennedy, P. C., Otterstedt, J., Baker, S. K., & Kame'enui, E. J. (2011). *DIBELS Data System: 2010–2011 Percentile Ranks for DIBELS Next Benchmark Assessments* (Tech. Rep. No. 1101). Eugene: University of Oregon.

Daniel, M. H. (2010). *Reliability of AIMSweb Reading Curriculum-based Measurement (R-CBM) (oral reading fluency).* Bloomington, MN: NCS Pearson. Available at *www.aimsweb.com.*

Davies, M., & Gardner, D. (2010). *A frequency dictionary of contemporary American English: Word sketches, collocates, and thematic lists.* New York: Routledge.

De La Paz, S., Owen, B., Harris, K. R., & Graham, S. (2000). Riding Elvis' motorcycle: Using self-regulated strategy development to plan and write for a state exam. *Learning Disabilities Research and Practice, 15,* 101–109.

Deno, S. L., Fuchs, L. S., Marston, D., & Shin, J. (2001). Using curriculum-based measurement to establish growth standards for students with learning disabilities. *School Psychology Review, 30,* 507–526.

Denton, C. A., & Vaughn, S. (2010). Preventing and remediating reading difficulties: Perspectives from research. In T. A. Glover & S. Vaughn (Eds.), *The promise of response to intervention: Evaluating current science and practice* (pp. 113–142). New York: Guilford Press.

Dolch, E. W. (1936). A basic sight vocabulary. *Elementary School Journal, 36,* 456–460.

Dorn, L. J., & Henderson, S. C. (2010). The comprehensive intervention model: A systems approach to RTI. In M. Y. Lipson & K. K. Wixson (Eds.), *Successful approaches to RTI: Collaborative practices for improving K–12 literacy* (pp. 88–120). Newark, DE: International Reading Association.

Dowhower, S. L. (1987). Effects of repeated reading on second-grade transitional readers' fluency and comprehension. *Reading Research Quarterly, 22,* 389–406.

Dunn, L. M., & Dunn, D. M. (2007). *Peabody Picture Vocabulary Test* (4th ed.). San Antonio, TX: Pearson.

Ehri, L. C. (1998). Grapheme–phoneme knowledge is essential for learning to read words in English. In J. L. Metsala & L. C. Ehri (Eds.), *Word recognition in beginning literacy* (pp. 3–40). Mahwah, NJ: Erlbaum.

Ehri, L. C., Dreyer, L. G., Flugman, B., & Gross, A. (2007). Reading Rescue: An effective tutoring intervention model for language-minority students who are struggling readers in first grade. *American Educational Research Journal, 44,* 414–448.

Espin, C. A., & Deno, S. L. (1993a). Content specific and general reading disabilities of secondary-level students: Identification and educational relevance. *Journal of Special Education, 27,* 321–337.

Espin, C. A., & Deno, S. L. (1993b). Performance in reading from content-area text as an indicator of achievement. *Remedial and Special Education, 14*(6) 47–59.

Espin, C. A., & Deno, S. L. (1994–1995). Curriculum-based measures for secondary students: Utility and task specificity of text-based reading and vocabulary measures for predicting performance on content-area tasks. *Diagnostique, 20,* 121–142.

Espin, C. A., Shin, J., & Busch, T. W. (2005). Curriculum-based measurement in the content areas: Vocabulary matching as an indicator of progress in social studies learning. *Journal of Learning Disabilities, 38,* 353–363.

Fountas, I. C., & Pinnell, G. S. (2006). *Leveled book list K–8.* Portsmouth, NH: Heinemann.

Fountas, I. C., & Pinnell, G. S. (2010). *Benchmark Assessment System* (2nd ed.). Portsmouth, NH: Heinemann.

Fry, E. (1980). The new Instant Word List. *The Reading Teacher, 34,* 284–289.

Fuchs D., Stecker, P. M., & Fuchs, L. S. (2008). Tier 3: Why special education must be the most intensive tier in a standards-driven, No Child Left Behind world. In D. Fuchs, L. S. Fuchs, & S. Vaughn (Eds.), *Response to intervention: A framework for reading educators* (pp. 71–104). Newark, DE: International Reading Association.

Fuchs, L. S., & Fuchs, D. (1992). Identifying a measure for monitoring student reading progress. *School Psychology Review, 21,* 45–58.

Fuchs, L. S., & Fuchs, D. (2004). *Using CBM for progress monitoring.* Retrieved from *www.studentprogress.org.*

Fuchs, L. S., Fuchs, D., & Hamlett, C. (2007). Using curriculum-based measurement to inform reading instruction. *Reading and Writing: An Interdisciplinary Journal, 20,* 553–567.

Fuchs, L. S., Fuchs, D., Hamlett, C. L., Walz, L., & Germann, G. (1993). Formative evaluation of academic progress: How much growth can we expect? *School Psychology Review, 22,* 27–48.

Ganske, K. (2000). *Word journeys: Assessment-guided phonics, spelling, and vocabulary instruction.* New York: Guilford Press.

Gersten, R., Compton, D., Connor, C. M., Dimino, J., Santoro, L., Linan-Thompson, S., et al. (2008). *Assisting students struggling with reading: Response to intervention and multi-tier intervention for reading in the primary grades: A practice guide* (NCEE No. 2009-4045). Washington, DC: National Center for Education Evaluation and Regional Assistance, Institute of Education Sciences, U.S. Department of Education. Retrieved from *http://ies.ed.gov/ncee/wwc/publications/practiceguides.*

Goeke, J. L., & Ritchey, K. D. (2008). Reconfiguring general and special education to meet the needs of struggling readers: The promise of response to intervention models. In S. B. Wepner & D. S. Strickland (Eds.), *The administration and supervision of reading programs* (4th ed., pp. 198–211). New York: Teachers College Press.

Goldman, S. R., Varma, K. O., Sharp, D., & Cognition and Technology Group at Vanderbilt. (1999). Children's understanding of complex stories: Issues of representation and assessment. In S. R. Goldman, A. C. Graesser, & P. van den Broek (Eds.), *Narrative comprehension, causality, and coherence: Essays in honor of Tom Trabasso* (pp. 135–159). Mahwah, NJ: Erlbaum.

Graham, S., & Harris, K. R. (1989). Improving learning disabled students' skills at composing essays: Self-instructional strategy training. *Exceptional Children, 56,* 201–216.

Graham, S., & Harris, K. R. (2003). Students with learning disabilities and the process of writing: A meta-analysis of the SRSD studies. In H. L. Swanson, K. R. Harris, & S. Graham (Eds.), *Handbook of learning disabilities* (pp. 323–344). New York: Guilford Press.

Hall, G. E., & Hord, S. M. (2006). *Implementing change: Patterns, principles, and potholes.* Boston: Pearson/Allyn & Bacon.

Hall, S. L. (2006). *I've DIBEL'd, now what?* Frederick, CO: Sopris West.

Harcourt Brace Educational Measurement. (2002). *Stanford Achievement Test* (10th ed.). San Antonio, TX: Pearson.

Harris, K. R., Graham, S., Mason, L. H., & Friedlander, B. (2008). *Powerful writing strategies for all students.* Baltimore: Brookes.

Hasbrouck, J., & Tindal, G. A. (2006). Oral reading fluency norms: A valuable assessment tool for reading teachers. *The Reading Teacher, 59,* 636–644.

Henderson, E. H. (1981). *Learning to read and spell: The child's knowledge of words.* DeKalb: Northern Illinois Press.

Hiebert, E. H., & Pearson, P. D. (2010). *An examination of current text difficulty indices with early reading texts* (Reading Research Rep. No. 10-01). San Francisco: TextProject. Retrieved from *http://textproject.org/research.*

Hintze, J. M., & Marcotte, A. M. (2010). Student assessment and data-based decision making. In T. A. Glover & S. Vaughn (Eds.), *The promise of Response to Intervention: Evaluating current science and practice* (pp. 57–77). New York: Guilford Press.

Hoffman, J. V., & Sailors, M. (2008). Evaluation and change: The role of the literacy specialist in guiding program improvement. In S. B. Wepner & D. S. Strickland (Eds.), *The administration and supervision of reading programs* (4th ed., pp. 231–253). New York: Teachers College Press.

Hord, S. (1986). *A manual for using innovation configurations to assess teacher development programs.* Austin, TX: Southwest Educational Development Laboratory.

Hosp, M. K., Hosp, J. L., & Howell, K. W. (2007). *The ABCs of CBM: A practical guide of curriculum-based measurement.* New York: Guilford Press.

Individuals with Disabilities Education Improvement Act of 2004, Public Law 108-466.

Invernizzi, M., & Hayes, L. (2004). Developmental-spelling research: A systematic imperative. *Reading Research Quarterly, 39,* 216–228.

Invernizzi, M., Swank, L., Juel, C., & Meier, J. (2007). *PALS-K: Phonological awareness literacy screening-kindergarten* (6th ed.). Charlottesville: University of Virginia.

Jacobs, J. E., & Paris, S. G. (1987). Children's metacognition about reading: Issues in definition, measurement, and instruction. *Educational Psychologist, 22,* 255–278.

Johns, J. L. (2011). *Basic Reading Inventory* (10th ed.). Dubuque, IA: Kendall-Hunt.

Juel, C. (1988). Learning to read and write: A longitudinal study of 54 children from first through fourth grades. *Journal of Educational Psychology, 80,* 443–447.

Karlsen, B., & Gardner, E. F. (1995). *Stanford Diagnostic Reading Test* (4th ed.). San Antonio, TX: Pearson.

Klauda, S. L., & Guthrie, J. T. (2008). Relationships of three components of reading fluency to reading comprehension. *Journal of Educational Psychology, 100*, 310–321.

Klingner, J. K., Vaughn, S., Arguelles, M. E., Hughes, T. J., & Leftwich, S. A. (2004). Collaborative strategic reading: "Real-world" lessons from classroom teachers. *Remedial and Special Education, 25*, 291–302.

Klingner, J. K., Vaughn, S., Hughes, M. T., Schumm, J. S., & Elbaum, B. (1998). Outcomes for students with and without learning disabilities in inclusive classrooms. *Learning Disabilities Research and Practice, 13*(3), 153–161.

Klingner, J. K., Vaughn, S., & Schumm, J. S. (1998). Collaborative strategic reading during social studies in heterogeneous fourth-grade classrooms. *Elementary School Journal, 99*, 3–22.

Kuhn, M. R., Schwanenflugel, P. J., & Meisinger, E. B. (2010). Aligning theory and assessment of reading fluency: Automaticity, prosody, and definitions of fluency. *Reading Research Quarterly, 45*, 230–251.

Lehr, F., Osborn, J., & Hiebert, E. H. (2004). *A focus on vocabulary* (ES0419). Honolulu, HI: Pacific Resources for Education and Learning.

Leslie, L., & Caldwell, J. S. (2010). *Qualitative Reading Inventory* (5th ed.). Boston: Allyn & Bacon.

Linan-Thompson, S., Cirino, P. T., & Vaughn, S. (2007). Determining English language learners' response to intervention: Questions and some answers. *Learning Disability Quarterly, 30*, 185–195.

Linan-Thompson, S., Vaughn, S., Prater, K., & Cirino, P. (2006). The response to intervention of English language learners at risk for reading problems. *Journal of Learning Disabilities, 39*, 390–398.

MacGinitie, W. H., MacGinitie, R. K., Maria, K., Dreyer, L. G., & Hughes, K. E. (2006). *Gates–MacGinitie Reading Test* (4th ed.). Itasca, IL: Riverside.

Machek, G. R., & Nelson, J. M. (2007). How should reading disabilities be operationalized?: Survey of practicing school psychologists. *Learning Disabilities Research and Practice, 22*, 147–157.

McKenna, M. C., & Layton, K. (1990). Concurrent validity of cloze as a measure of intersentential comprehension. *Journal of Educational Psychology, 82*, 372–377.

McKenna, M. C., & Picard, M. (2006/2007). Does miscue analysis have a role in effective practice? *The Reading Teacher, 60*, 378–380.

McKenna, M. C., & Stahl, K. A. D. (2009). *Assessment for reading instruction* (2nd ed.). New York: Guilford Press.

McKenna, M. C., & Walpole, S. (2005). How well does assessment inform our reading instruction? *The Reading Teacher, 59*, 84–86.

McKenna, M. C., & Walpole, S. (2008). *The literacy coaching challenge: Models and methods for grades K–8*. New York: Guilford Press.

McMaster, K., Fuchs, D., Fuchs, L. S., & Compton, D. L. (2002). Monitoring the academic progress of children who are unresponsive to generally effective early reading intervention. *Assessment for Effective Intervention, 27*(4), 23–33.

Mellard, D., McKnight, M., & Jordan, J. (2010). RTI tier structures and instructional intensity. *Learning Disabilities Research and Practice, 25*, 217–225.

Mesmer, H. A. (2001). Decodable text: A review of what we know. *Reading Research and Instruction, 40,* 462–483.

Miller, J., & Schwanenflugel, P. J. (2008). A longitudinal study of the development of reading prosody as a dimension of oral reading fluency in early elementary school children. *Reading Research Quarterly, 43,* 336–354.

Morris, R. D., Lovett, M. W., Wolf, M., Sevcik, R. A., Steinbach, K. A., Frijters, J. C., et al. (2012). Multiple-component remediation for developmental reading disabilities: IQ, socioeconomic status, and race as factors in remedial outcome. *Journal of Learning Disabilities, 45,* 99–127.

National Institute of Child Health and Human Development. (2000). *Report of the National Reading Panel. Teaching children to read: An evidence-based assessment of the scientific research literature on reading and its implications for reading instruction* (NIH Publication No. 00-4769). Washington, DC: U.S. Government Printing Office. Available at *www. nationalreadingpanel.org.*

Neuman, S. B. (2011). Single-subject experimental design. In N. K. Duke & M. H. Mallette (Eds.), *Literacy research methodologies* (2nd ed., pp. 383–403). New York: Guilford Press.

O'Connor, R. E., & Vadasy, P. F. (Eds.). (2011). *Handbook of reading interventions.* New York: Guilford Press.

Orosco, M. J., & Klingner, J. (2010). One school's implementation of RTI with English language learners: "Referring into RTI." *Journal of Learning Disabilities, 43,* 269–288.

Paratore, J. R., Steiner, L. M., & Dougherty, S. (2012). Developing effective home–school literacy partnerships. In R. M. Bean & A. Swan Dagen (Eds.), *Best practices of literacy leaders: Keys to school improvement* (pp. 317–336). New York: Guilford Press.

Paris, A. H., & Paris, S. G. (2003). Assessing narrative comprehension in young children. *Reading Research Quarterly, 38,* 36–76.

Paris, S. G. (2005). Reinterpreting the development of reading skills. *Reading Research Quarterly, 40,* 184–202.

Parker, R. I., & Hasbrouck, J. E. (1992). The maze as a classroom-based reading measure: Construction methods, reliability, and validity. *Journal of Special Education, 26,* 195–218.

Pearson, P. D., Hiebert, E. H., & Kamil, M. L. (2007). Vocabulary assessment: What we know and what we need to learn. *Reading Research Quarterly, 42,* 282–296.

Pedron, N. (1996). Reading Recovery: Implications for special education. *Special Services in the Schools, 12*(1–2), 49–59.

Peterson, B. (1991). Selecting books for beginning readers: Children's literature suitable for young readers. In D. E. DeFord, C. A. Lyons, & G. S. Pinnell (Eds.), *Bridges to literacy: Learning from Reading Recovery* (pp. 119–147). Portsmouth, NH: Heinemann.

Pinnell, G. S., Lyons, C. A., DeFord, D. E., Bryk, A. S., & Seltzer, M. (1994). Comparing instructional models for the literacy education of high-risk first graders. *Reading Research Quarterly, 29,* 8–39.

Rasinski, T., Rikli, A., & Johnston, S. (2009). Reading fluency: More than automaticity? Morethan a concern for the primary grades? *Literacy Research and Instruction, 48,* 350–361.

Read, C. (1971). Pre-school children's knowledge of English phonology. *Harvard Educational Review, 41,* 1–34.

Robinson, F. P. (1970). *Effective study* (4th ed.). New York: Harper & Row.

Samuels, S. J. (1979). The method of repeated readings. *The Reading Teacher, 32,* 403–408.

Sanetti, L. H., & Kratochwill, T. R. (2005). Treatment integrity assessment within a problem-solving model. In R. Brown-Chidsey (Ed.), *Assessment for intervention: A problem-solving approach* (pp. 304–325). New York: Guilford Press.

Scanlon, D. M., Anderson, K. L., & Sweeney, J. M. (2010). *Early intervention for reading difficulties: The interactive strategies approach.* New York: Guilford Press.

Schell, L. M., & Hanna, G. S. (1981). Can informal reading inventories reveal strengths and weaknesses in comprehension subskills? *The Reading Teacher, 35,* 263–268.

Shanahan, T., Callison, K., Carriere, C., Duke, N. K., Pearson, P. D., Schatschneider, C., et al. (2010). *Improving reading comprehension in kindergarten through 3rd grade: A practice guide* (NCEE No. 2010-4038). Washington, DC: National Center for Education Evaluation and Regional Assistance, Institute of Education Sciences, U.S. Department of Education. Retrieved from *whatworks.ed.gov/publications/practiceguides.*

Shananan, T., Kamil, M. L., & Tobin, A. W. (1982). Cloze as a measure of intersentential comprehension. *Reading Research Quarterly, 17,* 229–255.

Shapiro, E. S., Zigmond, N., Wallace, T., & Marston, D. (Eds.). (2011). *Models for implementing response to intervention: Tools, outcomes, and implications.* New York: Guilford Press.

Shin, J., Deno, S. L., & Espin, C. (2000). Technical adequacy of the maze task for curriculum-based measurement of reading growth. *Journal of Special Education, 34,* 164–172.

Shinn, M. R., & Shinn, M. M. (2002). *Administration and scoring of reading curriculumbased measurement (RCBM) for use in general outcome measurement.* Eden Prairie, MN: Edformation.

Silvaroli, N. J. (1976). *Classroom reading inventory.* Dubuque, IA: Kendall-Hunt.

6 + 1 Writing Trait® Rubric. Portland, OR: Education Northwest. Available at *http://education-northwest.org/resource/464.*

Stahl, K. A. D. (2009). Assessing the comprehension of young children. In S. E. Israel & G. G. Duffy (Eds.), *Handbook of research on reading comprehension* (pp. 428–448). New York: Routledge.

Stahl, K. A. D. (2011). Applying new visions of reading development in today's classrooms. *Reading Teacher, 65,* 52–56.

Stahl, K. A. D., & Bravo, M. A. (2010). Contemporary classroom vocabulary assessment for content areas. *The Reading Teacher, 63,* 566–579.

Stahl, K. A. D., & Keane, A. (2010, May). *A longitudinal investigation of response to intervention in an urban setting.* Paper presented at the annual meeting of the American Educational Research Association, Denver, CO.

Stahl, K. A. D., Keane, A., & Simic, O. (in press). Translating policy to practice: Initiating RTI in urban schools. *Urban Education.*

Stahl, S. A., & Heubach, K. (2005). Fluency-oriented reading instruction. *Journal of Literacy Research, 37,* 25–60.

Stahl, S. A., & Murray, B. A. (1994). Defining phonological awareness and its relationship to early reading. *Journal of Educational Psychology, 86,* 221–234.

Stahl, S. A., & Nagy, W. E. (2006). *Teaching word meanings.* Mahwah, NJ. Erlbaum.

Stanovich, K. E. (1980). Toward an interactive–compensatory model of individual differences in the development of reading fluency. *Reading Research Quarterly, 16,* 32–71.

Stanovich, K. E. (1986). Matthew effects in reading: Some consequences of individual differences in the acquisition of literacy. *Reading Research Quarterly, 21,* 360–407.

Stanovich, K. E. (2000). *Progress in understanding reading: Scientific foundations and new frontiers.* New York: Guilford Press.

Stenner, A. J., Burdick, H., Sanford, E. E., & Burdick, D. S. (2007). *The Lexile framework for reading* (Tech. Rep.). Durham, NC: Metametrics.

Taylor, B. M., Pearson, P. D., Clark, K., & Walpole, S. (2000). Effective schools and accomplished teachers: Lessons about primary grade reading instruction in low-income schools. *Elementary School Journal, 101,* 121–166.

Taylor, B. M., Peterson, D. S., Pearson, P. D., & Rodriguez, M. C. (2002). Looking inside classrooms: Reflecting on the "how" as well as the "what" in effective reading instruction. *The Reading Teacher, 56,* 70–79.

Topping, K. J. (1987). Paired Reading: A powerful technique for parent use. *The Reading Teacher, 40,* 608–609.

Topping, K. J., & Bryce, A. (2004). Cross-age peer-tutoring of reading and thinking: Influence on thinking skills. *Educational Psychology, 24,* 595–621.

Topping, K. J., Miller, D., Thurston, A., McGavok, K., & Conlin, N. (2011). Peer tutoring in reading in Scotland: Thinking big. *Literacy, 45*(1), 3–9.

Torgesen, J. K. (2000). Individual differences in response to early interventions in reading: The lingering problem of treatment resisters. *Learning Disabilities: Research and Practice, 15*(1), 55–64.

Torgesen, J. K., & Bryant, B. R. (2004). *TOPA-2+: Test of Phonological Awareness* (2nd ed.). Austin, TX: PRO-ED.

Torgesen, J. K., Wagner, R., & Rashotte, C. (1999). *Test of Word Reading Efficiency (TOWRE).* Austin, TX: PRO-ED.

Valencia, S. W., Smith, A. T., Reece, A. M., Min, L., Wixson, K., & Newman, H. (2010). Oral reading fluency assessment: Issues of construct, criterion, and consequential validity. *Reading Research Quarterly, 45,* 270–291.

Vannest, K. J., Parker, R., & Dyer, N. (2011). Progress monitoring in grade 5 science for low achievers. *Journal of Special Education, 44,* 221–233.

Vaughn, S., & Denton, C. A. (2008). Tier 2: The role of intervention. In D. Fuchs, L. S. Fuchs, & S. Vaughn (Eds.), *Response to intervention: A framework for reading educators* (pp. 51–70). Newark, DE: International Reading Association.

Vaughn, S., Gersten, R., & Chard, D. J. (2000). The underlying message in LD intervention research: Findings from research syntheses. *Exceptional Children, 67*(1), 99–114.

Vellutino, F. R., & Scanlon, D. M. (2002). The interactive strategies approach to reading intervention. *Contemporary Educational Psychology, 27,* 573–635.

Vellutino, F. R., Scanlon, D., & Lyon, G. R. (2000). Differentiating between difficult to remediate and readily remediated poor readers: More evidence against the IQ-discrepancy definition of reading disability. *Journal of Learning Disabilities, 33,* 223–238.

Vellutino, F. R., Scanlon, D. M., Sipay, E. R., Small, S., Chen, R., Pratt, A., et al. (1996). Cognitive profiles of difficult-to-remediate and readily remediated poor readers: Early intervention as a vehicle for distinguishing between cognitive and experiential deficits as basic causes of specific reading disability. *Journal of Educational Psychology, 88,* 601–638.

Wagner, R. K., Torgesen, J. K., & Rashotte, C. A. (1999). *Comprehensive Test of Phonological Processing (CTOPP).* Austin, TX: PRO-ED.

Walpole, S., & McKenna, M. C. (2007). *Differentiated reading instruction: Strategies for the primary grades.* New York: Guilford Press.

Walpole, S., & McKenna, M. C. (2009). *How to plan differentiated reading instruction: Resources for grades K–3.* New York: Guilford Press.

Walpole, S., & McKenna, M. C. (2012). *The literacy coach's handbook: A guide to research-based practice* (2nd ed.). New York: Guilford Press.

Walpole, S., McKenna, M. C., Coker, D. L., & Philippakos, Z. (2010, December). *A comparison of skills versus strategy instruction in first grade.* Paper presented at the annual meeting of the Literacy Research Association, Fort Worth, TX.

Walpole, S., McKenna, M. C., & Philippakos, Z. A. (2011). *Differentiated reading instruction in grades 4 and 5: Strategies and resources.* New York: Guilford Press.

Wanzek, J., & Vaughn, S. (2010). Research-based implications from extensive early reading interventions. In T. A. Glover & S. Vaughn (Eds.), *The promise of response to intervention: Evaluating current science and practice* (pp. 113–142). New York: Guilford Press.

Wanzek, J., & Vaughn, S. (2011). Is a three-tier reading intervention model associated with reduced placement in special education? *Remedial and Special Education, 32,* 167–175.

Williams, K. T. (2007). *Expressive Vocabulary Test* (2nd ed.). San Antonio, TX: Pearson.

Wixson, K. K., Lipson, M. Y., & Johnston, P. H. (2010). Making the most of RTI. In M. Y. Lipson & K. K. Wixson (Eds.), *Successful approaches to RTI: Collaborative practices for improving K–12 literacy* (pp. 1–19). Newark, DE: International Reading Association.

Wixson, K. K., & Valencia, S. W. (2011). Assessment in RTI: What teachers and specialists need to know. *The Reading Teacher, 64,* 466–469.

Wolf, M., Miller, L., & Donnelly, K. (2000). Retrieval Rate, Accuracy and Vocabulary Elaboration, Orthography (RAVE-O): A comprehensive, fluency-based reading intervention program. *Journal of Learning Disabilities, 33,* 375–386.

Wolf, M., & Segal, D. (1999). Retrieval Rate, Accuracy and Vocabulary Elaboration (RAVE) in reading-impaired children: A pilot intervention programme. *Dyslexia, 5,* 1–27.

Woodcock, R. W., McGrew, K. S., & Mather, N. (2001, 2007). *Woodcock Johnson III Normative Update Tests of Achievement.* Rolling Meadows, IL: Riverside.

Zigmond, N., & Kloo, A. (2012). The role of the special educator: A balancing act. In R. M. Bean & A. Swan Dagen (Eds.), *Best practices of literacy leaders: Keys to school improvement* (pp. 86–102). New York: Guilford Press.

Index

Page references in *italic* refer to figures and tables.